PERSC
GEOGR

ELIZABETH COATSWORTH

PERSONAL GEOGRAPHY

Almost an Autobiography

Foreword by

HELEN NEARING

The Countryman Press
WOODSTOCK, VERMONT

Countryman Classics are books of eloquence, charm, and
literary quality that our editors wish to restore to print in
affordable new editions, for the enjoyment of successive
generations of readers.

Copyright © 1976, 1977 by Elizabeth Coatsworth Beston
Foreword to this edition © 1994 by Helen Nearing

Personal Geography: Almost an Autobiography was first published by Stephen
Greene Press in 1976. First Countryman Press edition published in 1994.

Cover design by James F. Brisson
Cover photo by Tom Jones

Published by the Countryman Press, Inc.
PO Box 175
Woodstock, Vermont 05091

Printed in the United States of America

LIBRARY OF CONGRESS CATALOGING-IN-PUBLICATION DATA

Coatsworth, Elizabeth Jane, 1893-1986
    Personal geography : almost an autobiography / Elizabeth Coatsworth
p. cm.
Includes index.
ISBN 0-88150-300-2 : $13.00
1. Coatsworth, Elizabeth Jane, 1893-1986—Biography.
2. Women authors, American—20th century—Biography.
I. Title.
PS3505.O136Z52   1994
813'.52—dc20
[B]   94-29228
                                                       CIP

A Dedication

To three great editors:
Louise Seaman Bechtel of Macmillan,
the first editor of a children's department
in American book publishing; to Susan Hirschman of
Greenwillow Books, so unfailingly helpful over the years;
and to Janet Greene, who created this book from a mass of
materials as one might string a necklace from a bowl
overflowing with beads—to these among many
kind editors over the years I owe especial
gratitude and affection.

E.C.B.

Contents

ON THE CONTINENT

ON THE MEDITERRANEAN

IN THE EAST THAT LIES WEST

Journeys from Chimney Farm (1930–1968)

Journeys in My Mind (1968—)

I have always loved journeys
      long or short,
but this journey on which I shall
      some day embark—
is it long or short? No one
      seems to be able to tell me.

Foreword

I never met Elizabeth Coatsworth or Henry Beston, but almost did. I wangled an invitation for myself and a group of Vermont women fellow hillbillies. We were welcome, they told us, if we were content to sleep in the barn. We got set to go, but something now unknown intervened, and we never made the trip from Vermont to Maine.

Decades later I am asked to write of a woman I never met, and as I read her book *Personal Geography*, I find we had much in common. She grew up at the end of the last century in Buffalo, New York. I, in the beginning of the present century, was born in New York City and grew up in its suburbs. I started traveling the world at seventeen upon leaving high school and spent the next years in Europe, Asia and Australia. Elizabeth took her first trip abroad at the age of fifteen, and at twenty-three took an extensive trip to the Far East. We both married older, intellectual men who served as inspiration and teachers. We both (with little preparation) landed in a rural setting and adapted heartily to it, and we both remained there with our congenial husbands till their deaths. We continued on alone, in the country, in widowhood.

Elizabeth and I wrote—by hand, not on a machine. She was a poetic traveler, really "on pilgrimage," and she describes her sojourns movingly and with grace. Scott and I were more prosaic travelers, and while we experienced the beauties that we saw, we did not describe them in our books. The enchantment she found in dusty Macao and in the back streets of Budapest we missed in our search for statistics on students in schools and factory workers. Her aims and ours were different; ours on facts for further writing and Scott's lectures; hers on vignettes and personal reminiscences. Her book is full of poetic examples of these.

Elizabeth writes in *Personal Geography* that she is feeling her age at eighty-three, although noting that she "has been spared arthritis and most of the other painful companions of old age," as have I. She writes: "I still think; I still write; I still read; and still see my friends." As do I at age eighty-nine. I pass Elizabeth Coatsworth on with a friendly handshake and even a hug, and say, "we would have been friends."

HELEN NEARING
Harborside, Maine 1994

The bristlecone pine is supposed to be the oldest tree in the world, older than even the sequoia. One measures the age of a tree on a cross-section whose rings show the amount of growth which the tree enjoyed each year. There is a wide circle for good years, and a very narrow one, sometimes almost none at all, marks the years of drought. I know that we show no such physical proofs of our experience, but I think our lives are not unlike those of the trees. Some years are good years and we expand in them; some years are bad ones and the most we can do is to hold our own. But good or bad, like the trees we are still ourselves, growing out from the heartwood of our youth which I believe is a combination of our inheritance and our upbringing. Like the trees, we may be able to correct a bend or knothole which shows in youth; we may cover over the scar of an injury which however will always be there, though it may be hidden from sight.

I like this sense that all my life and experience is contained in me. I am a five-year-old child in Egypt, I am a schoolgirl in a very strict private school on Park Street in Buffalo, I roam the beaches of Lake Erie, barefoot all summer, I explore the winter country-side around Vassar more thoroughly than I do its curriculum, I go to the theatre and art shows in New York and climb California mountains; later I travel in the Far East and around the Mediterranean with a piercing pleasure (and as always the more uncomfortable trips, the more dangerous moments, are the most clearly remembered).

I settle with my mother in an eighteenth-century house in Hingham overlooking Boston Harbor (how I love that house!). By this time travel has jarred me into writing, and writing has become almost as much a part of me as eating or sleeping. Then in my mid-thirties I marry a man both handsome and perceptive, and we have two little girls and buy a Maine farm overlooking hayfields and a lake. Life never stops. The daughters grow up and marry, each has four children. My husband, who is five years older than I, begins the long struggle with old age and for years I fight that inevitably losing battle with him. He dies, and for eight years I have lived the diminished life of a widow, with one daughter living in Alaska and the other in California, but one or both visiting me each summer.

I am an old woman now, fighting my own losing battle with age, but with time to enjoy life along the way, as Henry always did. Naturally I think of death. I don't want to die because even in this narrower radius there are so many people and things still to enjoy. I do not fear death itself I think, but I often do not like its approaches. Only the other day I first formulated for myself the truism: "You cannot conquer death, but perhaps you can conquer the fear of it."

All these things and a thousand more are embodied in me, the good years and the bad, the wide rings of growth and the narrow. One's past is not something we leave behind, but something we incorporate. When I write a story for children I am a child, with perhaps a grownup person's powers of criticism (at least so I hope). When I lunch with a group of young middle-aged people, I feel no difference between us; when I walk in to my neighbor's, watching every step for fear I may trip on something (my sense of balance is irretrievably lost!), I greet her as an equal as she sits in a big chair tatting, with her walker in front of her. Outwardly I am eighty-three years old, but inwardly I am every age, with the emotions and experience of each period. The important thing is that at each age I am myself, just as you are yourself. During much of my life I was anxious to be what someone else wanted me to be. Now I have given up that struggle. I am what I am.

*   *   *

This book is an amalgam of things, never published before, that I wrote in my notebooks as long as fifty years ago or wrote especially for it in the past two years. Each piece is a moment in my life, caught in passing, and the result should be read as it was written: in snatches—picked up and put down, and I hope picked up again.

ELIZABETH COATSWORTH
Chimney Farm
June 1976

Journeys from My Middle East

1893–1914

᪵ I see the big living room at *Soldiers Place* in Buffalo with its many windows and folding doors, the dark oak paneling and the green tile fireplace, the carved Italian table with the brass student lamp in the center. In a corner near the front windows opposite the sofa and the glassed bookcases sits Grandmother Coatsworth in a big black leather chair. She is a large figure dressed in black with narrow lace collar and cuffs. Her face is massive and handsome, with an aquiline nose and a firm mouth with a jutting lower lip, and her pure white hair is twisted into a knot held with a silver hairpin of filigree work. Everything about her is in place. She is reading aloud to me a story from the St. Nicholas magazine and I am walking up and down, up and down on the Persian carpet before her, a child with dark hair cut in what was called a Dutch bob, with a plain dark little dress, and with hands clenched. I have heard the story before but that only makes the approaching climax more unendurable, and as I walk I murmur over and over in my speech which kept so long a hint of baby-talk, "Oh, this is too 'citing, this is too 'citing!"

MIDDLE EASTERN FAMILY

There is a Middle East in this country as surely as there is a Middle West, but it is not called by that name. It is an emotion rather than a nomenclature. Central and western New York know it, and upstate Pennsylvania and perhaps even western Massachusetts, all localities far from the sea, one remove from the earlier settlements and yet part of the seaboard states. The Middle East has had plenty of history, but it is a little blinded by the more layered histories of the coast and by the covered-wagon-frontier epic to the west.

When I was a girl in Buffalo—where I was born in 1893 and where we lived until 1912—little was ever told us about the past. If, as we drove old Dolly up Delaware Avenue, Father should remark, "When I was a boy, most of this was farmland beyond North Street," the muse of history had received as much of her due as she was likely to get.

As I look back on my upbringing I can see that it was a little unusual even then. Our family came in three layers, instead of the usual two of parents and children. We lived with our Grandmother Coatsworth in a wide-shingled house, one of the three in Buffalo designed by Henry Hobson Richardson, but how we came to have it is a mystery I cannot now solve. When it was built, Richardson was already dead, and it is hard to know how the plans reached Electa Coatsworth's architect. But they did, and it was a beautiful house, with wide lawns on either side and in front the elm-tree-bordered Soldiers Place, the circle where three parkways met. In due time Grandmother sold one side of our land to her niece, who with her husband and four children lived in an unspeakably dreary red-brick house designed by Frank Lloyd Wright; and a very gloomy house it was, with so deep a verandah and such wide eaves that the sun never reached any of the rooms. Some years later old Dr. Silas Hubbard and Mrs. Hubbard, who wore the only lace cap I ever saw in use, came to live there. They had three daughters and one son, Elbert, who became an extremely popular lecturer and writer. Grandmother never mentioned his name after it became known that he had acquired a mistress while still married (and it was one of the great love affairs of our time).

For a number of years we spent our summers at Bay Beach on the Canadian shore of Lake Erie not far from Buffalo. Here our family had four cottages on a sandy ridge covered with maple trees above a perfect crescent between the amusement park of Crystal Beach, to which steamers came from Buffalo several times a day, and Point Abino. The long hilly point had acres of woodland famous for their flowers, which long ago had been studied and described by a Frenchman named Abineau, for whom the point was named. Otherwise we seem always to have done a good deal of traveling. Before I was a year old I had spent a winter in California. Most of my fifth year was spent abroad. I scarcely remember England, but I have definite memories of the spa to which we went in Germany, and of how nasty the waters tasted, and of Switzerland and of Italy. The most vivid memories are of Vesuvius and then of Egypt, so strange and so different that when I went there again twenty-five years later it was as if I had been away only a few weeks.

It was as a freshman in high school that I was again taken to Pasadena. Father rented an ugly Victorian house in an orange grove on the unspoiled Arroyo Seco that he loved (where the Rose Bowl is now). We lived there for two years and I went to a long-vanished private school so different from the school in Buffalo that I never respected its teaching, perhaps because it was essentially amateur. I did like the motto: "Fais ce que doit, advienne que pourra," which I hope is right but I don't know. My French has grown very shaky.

Father really had a gift for choosing places to go to. One winter we spent four weeks—this time without Grandmother Coatsworth—in the old pre-revolutionary Mexico. It is surprising how many sites we explored, even Monte Alban, at that time not yet excavated except for one trench lined with ugly figures which they now say were of dead captives. It was my first long horseback ride and I loved seeing the world from the saddle. Next summer we spent a month at Catalina Island with a good deal of fishing for Father. I became seasick at the first opportunity so I didn't go with him. Besides, after catching one very small sunfish when I was little, I never wanted to kill anything again. I remember being proud of that sunfish and not even sorry for it, yet something in me said, "That will do," and it has done me for the rest of my life. Next we camped in the uncrowded Yosemite Valley and I climbed many of the trails. It was when I was at the top of the Yosemite Falls that I asked myself if I enjoyed climbing and answered, "No!" I never voluntarily climbed again.

After the next summer I was an upperclassman at the Buffalo Seminary, a tall, rather awkward, earnest, high-spirited sort of girl, for the first time perhaps a leader, but surely a very incomplete person, with all the assurance and the insecurity of the young.

INHERITANCE

I have loved, yes, loved, many parts of England, France, Scotland, and Ireland, Spain, and of course Italy, but for two I have the especial feeling of belonging. One is Edinburgh and the Lowlands of Scotland from which my grandfather Adam Reid emigrated and where my Great-aunt Helen continued to live all through my younger days. The other is that dale in northern England from which the Coatsworths came—some of them, that is, for others of the family are still there—near Middleton-in-Teesdale, which lies folded in by the moors in the Palatinate of Durham. The valley is chiefly known for having the highest waterfall in England, which comes tumbling down from the moors with great ale-colored violence. For a person who knows Niagara Falls and the Yosemite it seems small enough, but it has its own fame.

Middleton is much like any village in the north of England. Its charm lies mostly in its dale with the moors set high above it on three sides. From them one heard the curlews crying and the bleating of ewes calling their lambs. Small and snug in its hidden valley lies the dale of the Tee, very green and cultivated and scattered with white farmhouses. It was from one of these small houses that Tamar Kidd Coatsworth and her four married sons had emigrated to America in the hard times that followed the Napoleonic Wars. My particular ancestor was married to Mally Graham, a name that still goes on in the family.

They had a long and stormy passage which ended when the captain put them off at Anticosti Island in the Gulf of St. Lawrence. "But you were to take us to Toronto!" "I only agreed to take you to America. This is America," he said and sailed away. I have read an indignant letter telling of how they suffered from exposure and poor food, but most of all from the insatiable mosquitoes, until they could hail a coasting vessel to take them up the river.

Ultimately Tamar Kidd Coatsworth and two of her sons settled in the newly rebuilt town of Buffalo, burned by the British in the War of 1812. There as the young town prospered, the young men prospered, too. Recently a very distant relative whom I have never met, the last of a group of tenuous cousins, asked me if I should like to have Tamar's teapot, as she had no children to whom to leave it. It came only last year, a big round enamelware kitchen teapot, the very queen of kitchen teapots with a beautiful eighteenth-century high pewter top, spout and bands. It is large enough to have held the nine big cups of tea with which I hope the voyaging Coatsworths constantly regaled themselves.

It was as I began to piece together a little of the family history that I found that only Grandmother Coatsworth came from stock that had been in this country since the seventeenth century. Her mother was a Hubbard from a line which came to Haddam, Connecticut, in 1635, I think. Later they married into the prolific stock of Simon Willard, through whom I have a very slender relationship to half the inhabitants of New England. I remember being at a dinner party many years ago at which several guests came from Connecticut, and they happened to say that anyone descended from a settler who had come to that colony before 1700 had Indian blood, because no English women were brought there before the eighteenth century. I used to think it would be romantic to trace the Indian ancestresses but the book of Hubbard genealogies is very reticent. All the wives, even the early ones, are named Deborah or Dorcas or Patience with English surnames, which of course doesn't mean that one or two of them were not originally Flying Bird or Two Deer. But if so, the record is lost to my casual reading.

Grandmother Coatsworth came to Buffalo as a bride, but she had been born and bred in western New York, beyond Hamburg in the rich orchard and grape country. Her name was Electa. She was the eldest of eight children.

I know so few details! At sixteen Grandmother was a tall, dark girl, who taught school to help earn a little money for that large household. The years went by and Electa Weller was twenty—twenty-five—twenty-eight. She was handsome and serious: she had shared with her mother the task of raising seven younger boys and girls on a farm without a man. Perhaps she had little time for sweethearts. Perhaps she had little taste for them. But one Sunday morning in spring found her in the village church, wearing a bonnet with roses under the brim. She was singing in the choir; her grave and lovely face was framed in roses. And a certain rising young merchant of Buffalo named Thomas Coatsworth, who had come to the settlement on business, watched her instead of the minister all during the service.

The year after her marriage she bore him twins, a dark-haired boy, William, and a girl, Mally, with the pink-and-white skin, fair hair and bright blue eyes of the north of England. She had two more children, a Caleb with his father's big hazel eyes and English look, and a dark Jenny, her darling. In fact, it was the shy ones whom she loved best. The others could fend for themselves: they were gay and outgoing, liked everyone and were liked by everyone. But the dark children loved books and to be by themselves. They were thoughtful and artistic. William would write a little when he left school, until the unwelcome responsibilities of business came to him in his twenties upon his father's death. Jenny would be one of the earliest students at Radcliffe; she would study singing in Paris, try sculpture, and travel, never quite finding the expression for her spirit which she needed.

When I knew her, Grandmother Coatsworth was a matriarch who made decisions and saw that they were carried out. When she went driving she carried a little black silk parasol that could be adjusted to any angle to its handle. She read me infinite numbers of stories of all sorts, but with the terrible snobbishness of children I was embarrassed because she used such old-fashioned words as "shears" and pronounced "wound" (an injury) to rhyme with "sound."

Every evening Grandmother, Mother and Father played casino until nine o'clock, when she said goodnight and went to bed. Somewhere, along with Methodism, Grandmother had left her fear of cards behind her.

So she lived, always dignified, always dominant, filled with long years and memories I was too young to share.

* * *

I am more nearly connected in time with my forebears in Scotland. There my great-grandfather James Reid lived and was a "publisher"—of what, I wonder? I never asked. In those days it was the present and future which seemed important; the past was a mere humus. But I do know that he was a stern man married to a "saint," and that they had several children, all of whom died of tuberculosis except for Adam, my grandfather, and his sister, my Great-aunt Helen. When Adam came of age he asked his father for a latchkey and his father said, "Never!" so the boy bought a ticket and sailed for Canada and in Toronto met and married sixteen-year-old Elizabeth Hugill, my mother's mother.

I can remember when Grandfather Reid died because I waited to be dressed in solid black like children in the books I read; but I never was, and wasn't even taken to the funeral—the first time I dimly recognized how different life is from fiction. I don't actually remember him, but he was a lion-headed man, and knew a great deal of poetry by heart, especially, I imagine, Burns and

Scott. He was something of an inventor, too, and invented the postbox with its lid falling over the letter-slit. The government had no wish for postboxes at the time and he copyrighted the idea. Later my rather happy-go-lucky bachelor uncle, Frank, let the copyright run out and a few months later postboxes appeared all over the country after a gleaner of old copyrights took up the idea, then timely.

Aunt Helen Reid was my first correspondent. I remember sitting uncomfortably at Mother's big desk writing letters to her on my child's notepaper, and of how promptly she replied. There was one phrase which she used that I loved. When she was going to move to other lodgings she would write, "I think I will flit next Lady's Day," which was the first of May. It was many years before I heard a word which gave me the same emotion as Aunt Helen's "flit," and that was Henry's when he referred to a fall, however painful, as a "toss." "I stumbled over the railroad tracks in the dark and had a terrible toss," he might say.

My sister, Margaret, and I were not as close to the Coatsworths as to the Reids. We were the only children in that family. There was Grandmother Reid and her daughter, Aunt Nelly, married to Uncle George Chester, and Uncle Frank Reid who never married but lived with Grandmother. To all four of these people we were as important as they were to us. There was an unspoken hostility between them and most of the Coatsworths, especially Aunt Mally (who married Herbert Lord, head of the philosophy department at Columbia), for she was a very dominant personality with whom they had gone to school. These things were never spoken of, but we felt them.

How complicated all family strains are! I suppose almost all blood goes blindly on, under different names, different circumstances. It's almost frightening to think of what complexities of inheritance we each are born with.

THE OPAL

Most artists, painters, writers, musicians, potters, and probably cabinetmakers are ruthless to themselves and others. Perhaps in the Nineties most heads of families were ruthless too. How else did Father decide to go home to Buffalo from a winter in Pasadena by way of an excursion up the Pacific Coast to Washington, stopping to see Uncle Frank Reid who was homesteading on Lake Cushman, high in the Olympics—and next pausing at a whistle-stop where there was not even a platform but where a carryall of some sort met him and his mother, and his wife, and lively four-year-old Margaret, and one-year-old Bess (that was me, and I was always seasick on long drives), and a nurse named Blanche and the unborn baby whom Mother was carrying, to drive out to see a Blackfoot encampment of tepees somewhere on the limitless plains east of the mountains?

If that didn't take ruthlessness in a man, what would? But Father never thought of it as anything but an opportunity to see something interesting. Years afterwards when I asked Mother about this and later trips, and of how she and Father dared to take such young children on such journeys, she replied with her usual serenity, "In those days people didn't consider the children first of all in doing anything. They made their own plans and the children went along." I knew Father for eighteen years and he was anything but a selfish man. He was loving and considerate, but, like a ship's captain, he was at the helm. And that was where everyone thought he ought to be.

I think it was in Seattle on our roundabout trip back to Buffalo that Father and Mother stood for some time looking at an exhibit of opals in a jewelry-store window. Considered unlucky, opals were then not widely used and Father had become interested in them during a winter in Mexico. My parents did not go into the store at the time, but, once home in Buffalo, Father kept thinking about a certain opal which had caught his fancy in Seattle. He didn't know the name of the store but he thought he remembered the name of the street it was on. To this uncertain address he wrote, describing the exact location in the display window of the desired stone; in due time he received an answer and later the opal, which he had set in an oval of small diamonds as a ring for Mother.

Mother wore it for some years without incident, and then one September afternoon at Bay Beach she looked down at her finger and saw the diamonds but not the opal they clasped. She searched about the floors, and then along the back path where that afternoon she had walked up to Aunt Nelly's for tea. No stone appeared among the grasses. She searched the round bathroom which formed the base of our little tower in the cottage, for she had washed her hair earlier, but she found no sign of the opal there. Such a stone isn't easy to find in grass: it isn't easy to find in sand, either, and our verandah and the adjoining platform under the maples were full of cracks.

The opal was given up for lost, but later that fall Uncle Caleb, who was staying at Bay Beach after we had left, "put up" for the winter Grandmother Coatsworth's cottage next to ours, and while draining the pipes he borrowed a sponge from our open cellar.

As he squeezed out the water something made a small tap at his feet and looking down he saw an opal. He had a vague idea that his sister-in-law had lost an opal, and so he put it into his vest pocket, where he promptly forgot its existence.

No one saw the stone again until he and Aunt Ruth were home in Atlantic City and she was going through the pockets of an old suit she meant to hand over to the rag man. That night at dinner she asked Uncle Caleb how he happened to have opals loose in his pocket, and he remembered its story.

A cousin was visiting in Atlantic City and was soon leaving for Buffalo. "And she'll take it back," said Aunt Ruth. "It will be much safer."

Aunt Ruth was mistaken, for the cousin lost her purse on a Buffalo streetcar on the day of her return. She advertised in the papers but had no response. When no answer came she telephoned Mother, and Mother for a second time bade the opal farewell.

Then on a Sunday a man appeared at the cousin's door. He was a workingman, he explained. He had found the purse, and read the advertisement, but he had had no free time to come until his Sunday holiday.

Early Monday morning the cousin rang our doorbell.

"Ida, here's your opal. I didn't dare keep it another twenty-four hours for fear something else would happen to it."

But apparently the opal had had its fling. It was returned to its ring and is still being worn, and seems to behave as well as any other stone.

FOUR MEMORIES OF CHILDHOOD

I

I am I then, much as I am now; the kernel was the same although there must have been fewer husks. I am sitting, happy, on Mother's lap. Perhaps there is a vague memory of her pince-nez eyeglasses. Then something comes hurtling across the floor towards us. I watch its sinister crab like motion. I see it approach nearer and nearer, it pulls itself upright holding to Mother's dress, it seems to me no better than a small ogre.

Mother lifts me down to the floor and picks up the creature, which even now seems to me to be holding its breath, red-faced, horribly determined. It is my baby sister, "Hubba," a little over a year younger than I. I know that I make no protest but sit forlornly on the floor, my sense of a secure universe shaken, my eyes focused with miserable intentness upon a square black firescreen with two owls embroidered on it.

Jealousy—it was not that. People do not understand that at such a moment an entire step away from babyhood must be taken, as drastic as when later a child first leaves the shelter of home.

II

The candle has been blown out, darkness closes over the room, but the stories told around the bonfire on the beach have not been blown out. In Buffalo the gas jet in the adjoining bathroom is always turned low at night, so a little girl need not go to sleep in utter darkness. But here in the country when the candle is blown out, it is blown out. If she wakes in the morning early she will find the sun streaming through the windows and turning the knot-holes of the unstained wood to a resinous rose, but now there is only blackness and the slight lisping of tideless waves.

One story above all others haunts me: the story of the man who was found murdered with four candles burning about him. When the detectives came they found only curious round marks in the earth outside and in the dust of the windowsill, but at length it was discovered that a monkey had been the killer, a monkey with pincushions fastened to its feet. The crouching terrified part of a child's mind heard a rustle in the thicket of chokecherries outside, heard a curious scraping along the wall, stared aghast at the open windows. The civilized part of the mind argued, "But there aren't any monkeys around here."

"There *might* be," whispered the other. "How can you *tell?*" Any moment something blacker than blackness might hunch across the sill, blotting out the starlight. A scream wouldn't be heard downstairs. Or perhaps one couldn't scream.

"But a monkey wouldn't tie pincushions ——"

"But there might be a monkey who *would* ——"

To be murdered by a monkey! A monkey with a knife. There was something worse than violent death about that; and vaguely the mind felt that the lighted candles set decently in pairs were after all only an added horror.

"There *couldn't* be ——"

"There *might* ——"

And so at last she falls asleep, in the grip of ancestral fears, the deep subconscious self within her having evoked the mood of tenseness and suspense that many a long-ago ancestress must have felt lying close to a fire with death prowling in the darkness beyond.

III

My next really complete memory is two and a half years later, although there are small glimpses between—the iron fence and slope between our house and Aunt Mally's on Cottage Street; the thimble hidden in a candlestick in the saloon of the cattle-boat on which we crossed the Atlantic, on the occasion of my fifth birthday; the delicious feel of catching hold of Mother's voluminous skirts to be pulled upstairs after a long day of sightseeing; the German countess throwing bonbons wrapped in bright colors from her window to us children on the lawn; an early morning in Switzerland when we were above the clouds and saw the sun rise; the smell of Egyptian tangerines. But always the pictures grow clearer as we go south on our year of travel, until I come to the sharply drawn scene that used occasionally to return as a dream.

The country is flat and dusty, with flat green fields and a straight road. I am on a donkey, and the patent-leather belt of my scarlet jacket is fastened about the pommel to give me a sense of greater security. The donkey-boy, barefooted, in a single long garment, runs beside us, urging the donkey on. I feel alone, alone with the donkey and the donkey-boy and Egypt. We meet men in blue, and their women with their eyes showing above black veils. I know that I bowed to them and I think they gave me some sort of greeting. That was all, but it was the first of many hours that were to come when my heart seemed too large for its cage of ribs with the joy and adventure of entering into a strange land.

IV

A picture has fallen from among the others, out of its place. It could be marked THE FIRST AWARENESS OF A SECRET MAGIC IN

NATURE and shows a tall girl, perhaps in her late teens, wandering alone back of the Bay Beach cottages that line the crescent of shore along the wide expanses of Lake Erie where she has spent most of her summers. She is visiting her aunt and uncle. It is autumn and she has set out to walk in the Paisley-shawl brilliance of the marshes behind the houses. Chance and one of the few roads of the place lead her to a sugarbush. The leaves of the maples are all a golden red, almost of one tone. The late afternoon light shines upon them and the columned trunks. There is no wind.

Then she sees that all the grove is filled with butterflies, the common monarch butterfly she has often seen hovering on milkweed or tipping on the black edge of a marsh rut. But now there are hundreds upon hundreds of them, just the color of the sugar maples' leaves, filling the air, lighting on the branches, fluttering and floating all about her. Have the leaves taken on life? Or are the maples clothed in butterflies?

It is perhaps the silence that fills her with a sense of having profaned (or was it shared?) a mystery.

MY MOTHER'S MIRROR

The walls of my room would be covered with portraits if only I knew the spell to call them forth from my mother's mirror with its round silver frame. The first portrait would perhaps be of Mother in her wedding veil, tucking orange blossoms between veil and soft fair hair. There would be many quick sketches of Mother later, in the first frilled shirtwaist, wearing for the first time her gold pince-nez, and then as an older woman, holding the same sweet look she had had as a girl. Father was not one to look much in mirrors, but he may have looked in this once or twice to see if the part in his hair was straight. There would be hidden here no portraits or sketches of Grandmother Coatsworth. She would, I think, never have entered her daughter-in-law's room. A young woman has a right to some privacy, and if Mother's was minimal, at least I am sure it was absolute.

Of course there would have been many sketches of Margaret and of me, so unalike in everything but our youth. The only carefully studied mirror-portrait of me was taken when I was ten or twelve years old.

Mother came into the room and said mildly, "You've looked long enough at yourself, Betty." Or was I still "Bess" then? Anyway she was completely mistaken. I was not admiring myself. I was searching to find out who and what I was. There was no humor in the eyes that looked back at me under the arching brows, but I am sure there was humor in the thoughts back of the eyes. Like Father, I could make a joke without smiling. Like him, I could not laugh, just as I could not whistle or sing. As yet no one even guessed when I thought something was funny.

So if I knew the magic formula, all about this room there would be sketches and sometimes portraits of us all, of blue-eyed, smiling Margaret, and of sober, solemn Betty dark as a shadow. Our spirits did not know then how akin they were, how in later years the fair and the dark would merge into one complete whole, which even death would not completely destroy.

MOTHER TELLS A LIE

If Grandmother Reid with her quick slim ways and her dark bright eyes and her love for flowers and fruits and birds reminded one of a jenny wren, Mother was more like a song sparrow, or perhaps a dove. She was round and sweet and very feminine. She was kind and friendly and admired other people and seemed scarcely to think of herself at all. She was cheerful and gentle, and never sat in judgment on anyone, but behind all this modesty and domesticity there was an absolute courage.

Not many years ago Father's sister, Aunt Mally, who with the mellowing years had become a true and dear friend to Mother, told me about going in to see the young Ida just after her first child—a son—was born dead. Mother had gone through a terrible protracted childbirth and finally to save her the child had to be taken. Aunt Mally said that Mother lay with her head over the side of the bed, more dead than alive, but she looked up at her young sister-in-law as she entered.

"I shall have a baby next year," she whispered, and she did.

In the years to come Margaret and I were to see her courage more than once. We could sense it when our little sister died of what was called "summer complaint" in her second year. Much later we took it for granted when we traveled together through the Far East and found ourselves (unvaccinated) in smallpox epidemics, and unarmed in the midst of some very lonely places. Mother stayed in Baguio while Margaret and I took a ten-day horseback trip alone through the head-hunting mountain country with two little Filipino boys and several Igorot carriers. One of the ladies at the mountain capital asked Mother if she were not worried with us gone for days, and hearing no word of us.

"Oh no," said Mother. "I always think if anything bad happens one learns about it somehow. So when I hear nothing I take it for granted that all is going well."

But the time that I look back upon with something approaching awe, was much earlier, while I was a senior at the Buffalo Seminary. Father, who had an instinct for such things, had found a lot on the stream below the old mill at Williamsville, perhaps ten miles outside the Buffalo city limits. There was a garage on it which had been fitted up temporarily with rooms: a living room with a couch, a little bedroom, and a very small kitchen with a door opening near the sink. The big garage doors were glassed like French windows and were kept closed. They lighted the living room.

Perhaps this may sound attractive. I don't think it was. The cottage-garage was a makeshift place but it served our purpose very well. It was the land about it that we loved, which was hilly at the back and covered with little black-stemmed wild plum trees filled in their season with white blossoms. Elms grew on the flat land above the stream, which ran here between little cliffs of shale. We had a headland, no larger than a big Persian carpet and just as flat, which for some reason jutted out into the stream and commanded a charming prospect of its course and of the meadows opposite.

All this ragged Paradise lay at the edge of Williamsville and was surrounded by an old board fence in which the boys had made a few gaps. There were no neighbors of any kind except for one cottage farther downstream, entirely out of sight and sound of ours and like ours only occasionally occupied.

In those days most families had cars, but one must have lived then to remember how gingerly they had to be used. The roads were still dirt lanes and we wore veils to keep the worst of the dust from our faces and eyes. The cars were prone to sudden colics and their tires punctured at the slightest excuse. Garages and mechanics were rare; any trouble was something of a catastrophe.

So Williamsville, on its flat road, only a little way from the city, with a streetcar occasionally jouncing along over grass-grown ties, was an excellent choice for a country seat. We used to drive out as a family for a picnic or tea over the millstream. And I used to love to bring a friend there for the weekend with some older person as chaperone.

On this spring Sunday there were three of us in the cottage washing the dishes in the teacup-sized kitchen, a sort of small entry with its three doors, one opening outdoors, one into the small bedroom and one into the main room.

I don't think that we two who were girls quite understood the possibilities when a man appeared at the outer door, which stood open, and asked in a surly voice to see "the mister." The stranger was the old-fashioned type of tramp, unshaven, bleary-eyed, with a cur's air of being both cowardly and dangerous.

Mother gave him one glance from her mild blue eyes and put another dripping dish in the dryer.

"My husband's taking a nap," she said with the slightest gesture of her head towards the half-opened door of the bedroom.

"I want to see him," the man repeated.

Mother spoke still very low. "I wouldn't think of waking him," she told the tramp. "You had better go away."

And perfectly serenely she went on washing dishes.

For a minute or two the creature hesitated, taking in her indifferent little figure only a foot or two away on the other side of the screen, and our young presences beyond. But there was the half-open door to the bedroom and the possible man behind it. By good fortune the curtains of the bedroom were so thick that the tramp had not been able to see through into the room as he passed by.

So he hesitated, a dark and ugly cloud, trying to make up his mind if Mother had told him the truth or not, but he could not be sure. Finally he gave a sort of grunt and went on. We heard his footsteps circling the house and caught a glimpse of him at the windows of the larger room. Mother went on rinsing out her dishpan and hanging up her dishcloth.

And the tramp left.

And later we all went out to sit in the spring sunshine on our little headland.

Now as I look back upon that five minutes I am struck with wonder at Mother's unperturbed manner, and more still at her quickness of wit. She estimated the danger and countered it. I can never remember her telling another lie in all the years that I knew her. But the really remarkable fact was that when the tramp was gone, she said nothing which could frighten two young and impressionable girls. She treated the incident as nothing at all, as though one had shooed out an old cat with a torn ear, or had flapped one's apron at a collarless dog. Whatever she may have felt, she kept serenely to herself.

AT GLEN IRIS

Occasionally an experience rounds into a kind of perfection, something lovely and unmarred to which one may look back with delight for the rest of one's life. Such was my first visit to the estate of William Pryor Letchworth, the nineteenth-century philanthropist from Buffalo and collector of Indian antiquities. I was young, and visiting a friend in East Aurora. She suggested that we might spend a weekend at Letchworth Park, twenty or thirty miles to the east at Portage. I think we took a train and then walked. I remember a steep hill and later a long railroad bridge over the Genesee and what had once a walkway, two boards wide and with a single handrail, by the side of the bridge over the river. The water ran swift and wide far, far below, a constant motion all too visible under one's feet. It was such a walk as only cats should try, and nothing in recent years would induce me to cross on it. But we were young and enjoyed adventure.

Beyond we could look down on the great estate of Glen Iris with its lawns, scattered trees and woodlands. The house had been built about the time of the Civil War and had tall Greek columns across the front, with a little balcony upstairs opening from the bridal chamber. One entered, we were to discover, by a side door near a pool large enough to have held, in its romantic youth, a little skiff wherein a lady might float with a sweetheart on a moonlit night.

The house only recently had been given to the state and few people knew of it. My friend and I were the only guests. We chose the best room, with its prints of Victorian Europe and its small stool upholstered in cross-stitch and its balcony with a view of the spray of falls rising in a lovely curtain beyond the green of the lawn. Beyond it again lay the forests and their wandering paths, famous in the spring for their wildflowers. We explored them at the edge of shale cliffs overhanging the rush of water. There were three falls, beautiful and enchanted. No one was ever in sight as we sat on the lawns to watch the first, or climbed down flights of stairs to see the last one boil into its cauldron of rock. That lovely turmoil, that blown and rainbowed wetness, were not then marred by picnic tables and rubbish containers. We had it all, unspoiled as when Mr. Letchworth had laid out his grounds for the pleasure of his guests. For us, day after day dawned clear and windless, or that is how I remember them: October at its brightest and most benign.

Have I given any feeling of the quality of this place, Victorian, romantic, far off from any world I knew? But to this wild and natural beauty contrasted with the charm of the mansion, there was a further overtone.

One evening in the library we picked up *The Narrative of the Life of Mary Jemison*, "the White Woman of the Genesee." In 1755, when she was about twelve years old and living on the frontier of Pennsylvania, she was taken captive by a foraging band of Indians and Frenchmen. Mary was adopted by two Seneca women living on the Ohio River. In due time she married an Indian and, with her first baby on her back, journeyed six hundred miles to the main hunting-grounds of the Seneca on the Genesee River. There she lived for most of her life, refusing, as an older woman, to leave the Indians to take up life again with the whites. At the council of chiefs she was given a tract of open land, called the Gordon Tract, which ran for six miles along the flats below the falls. Here for many years Mary Jemison lived, welcoming all who came to her in distress, until at last she became almost a legendary figure and in 1823 a Mr. James Seaver came to her expressly to take down the account of her life and adventures. On the hill above the Letchworth mansion stands a statue of her as a girl with her papoose strapped to her back. The house she built for her daughter has been moved beside it, along with the last of the Long Houses of the Six Nations. Here in the Council House one can see the bench built along the log walls where the chiefs sat, and the clay-and-stick chimneys at each end, and the fireplaces in which the council fires burned.

Here one feels the presence of the Indians in the days of their power, when their aid was sought by empires, and the council fire was more than a symbol. Yet Little Beard, Cornplanter, and the other chiefs are overshadowed by the short stalwart figure of Mary Jemison, the fabled white woman of the Genesee, who, in the midst of war and conflict, never lost her courage nor her sense of pity, and while refusing to leave her children and her adopted people, yet served as best she might the men of her own race.

FIRST INDEPENDENCE

Just now Mrs. Ball brought my breakfast tray to me as I sat on the open porch overlooking the pond, and said that this is the twenty-first birthday of Eric, our morning gardener.

"I'm glad it's not mine!" I exclaimed, yet thinking it over I am less sure. How many happy days have lighted up the years! But my life is now like a very thick book: one would hesitate to pick it up to begin it from the beginning, and read through to whatever the end will be.

Although this is not my twenty-first birthday, still I can remember my twenty-first year as if I were living it. It was my first year after graduating from Vassar and I was living alone in New York, taking a Master's degree at Columbia. I lived in two rooms (with "bath and kitchen privileges") in an apartment belonging to a school teacher. She must have had very different hours from mine because I seldom remember meeting her even in the hallway, and the kitchen I used only for making an eggnog which I

drank with my two rolls for breakfast, for I still had not learned
to like tea or coffee. The pint of milk was left each morning at
the door and the eggs and rolls I bought at a nearby grocery every
few days. My sharpest remembrance of the place is the pleasure
of feeling my independence and the mysterious passing of the
lighted elevated cars along the roofs below me at night. I was so
unsophisticated, or perhaps genuine, as to think that they were
beautiful. Even their roar I accepted as a dragon's roar.

I lived on an allowance which I never overspent, and sometimes I would be left with perhaps eighty-three cents for Sunday,
and lunch and supper might cost only twenty or thirty cents each,
which—heaven help us!—seemed adventurous in those days. I explored the city either alone or with a boy with whom I had grown
up during the long lakeshore summers. He was an incipient sci-
entist and was spending a year in New York. We walked in Van
Cortland Park, we visited half a dozen historic mansions; we
went to Fraunces Tavern, where Washington bade farewell to his
officers; we saw the last horsecars in New York (this was in 1916),
we stared at the city's skyline from the crown—or was it the
torch?—of the Statue of Liberty; we took a ferry across the Hud-
son and walked along the Palisades: and all of these things gave
me far more pleasure than did my four courses, which I often
skipped to spend long weekends with a former roommate in
Philadelphia.

I remember only one thing from a lecture by that Robinson
who wrote the then standard *European History and Reader* and
who was giving a crowded course in the history of the intellectual
classes in Europe. "If you are naturally conservative," he said, "do
not be ashamed of it. A civilization needs a heavy anchor to keep
it steady in the winds of change." Then there were the fervid
arguments on religion with a tall young Episcopal rector after or
before the course on Dante we were taking with Professor
Fletcher (I wrote a play laid in Renaissance Florence as my thesis,

which he accepted and which I suppose is still lying somewhere in the immense archives of Columbia). The course that I remember with most pleasure was Comparative Religion, given at eight o'clock in the evening by a young Canadian in the cellar of the Columbia library. *Pagan Christs* was among the books we read, and the religions we studied were the Mediterranean ones; there was a rabbi in the course and perhaps only ten or eleven of us in all. There was something clandestine about it: that after-sessions journey past the furnace rooms, that small classroom, the only one occupied at so late an hour, yet the general air of a secret meeting in the catacombs gave a sauce to the excellent teaching and discussion. It is still something of a mystery to me why a class should have been held at that time, in that place.

In the second semester my mother and sister came back from a trip to Alaska and took an apartment in New York, and I joined them. It was pleasant but less of an adventure. We saw more of relatives and the theatre, and I did less exploring. I no longer went down the menu of cheap restaurants picking out a twenty-five-cent meal. I still skipped classes, but visited in Philadelphia less often. I was taking a Master's degree for no especial reason, and that was about all there was to it.

THE UNCERTAIN MUSE

Glancing over my notebooks of poetry I find a whole series
written at Bay Beach one autumn after we had come back from
thirteen months' traveling leisurely and according to our whims
up and down the fabulous coasts of the Far East. And they were
fabulous in those days. I am a little saddened to remember the
strange and wonderful things we did in places which can never
again regain their ancient serenities. That fall I had come on
from California alone and was spending some weeks with Uncle
George and Aunt Nelly Chester in a landscape transformed by a
beautiful autumn. I was beginning to write poetry and to publish
it. *The Dial*, and Francis Hackett of *The New Republic* above
all, were giving me a steady and patient encouragement, slowly
teaching me the attitudes of the professional.

I know so little poetry that has been written describing the
Buffalo countryside, that I am jotting down half a dozen of my
early poems here. The first, which I called "On the Road to
Eden," came after a walking trip with friends:

Trellised grapevines shall be our walls with the patterned
         interweaving of leaves and tasseled spheres,
and the broad down-curving thatch of an apple tree
         shall roof us,
with the apples like little round lanterns, honey-colored,
         blurred with cerise,
swung to the rafters over our heads.

We shall have a great sunflower on its stalk
         for a grandfather's clock,

and if you miss a glimpse of the sea,
we can plant a strip of cabbages along the horizon
to refresh our eyes with their cool, frosted green.

Here is one called "September" that Aunt Nelly liked:

Shadows across the road as lavender
as the massed asters where the breezes stir
(sun, sun, and shadows like flowers).

Moths and bright butterflies flickering pair by pair
the little weeds and flowers of the air
(flying blossoms in sun-drenched hours).

Fat bees at worship of a meadow god
in the pagodas of the goldenrod
(gold priests droning from high gold towers
to the one
Great God, the Sun,
whose voice is song, and whose breath is flowers).

It is only a list without even a main verb, but it did get a little of
the sense of joy one felt on the Marsh Road at that time of year
when the weather was perfect.

When October came the glory of the maples seems to have
given my thought and pen no rest. I wrote a dozen poems about
them and compared them with everything. Here are two short
sketches:

The gold-bronze cockerel wood
with its arrogant comb of red maple
and spurs of sumac
seems about to crow
and clap its wings in defiance
of the other wood across the stacked cornfield.

The other one was about the Marsh Woods themselves, between the lake and the first farms:

No wind, no sound, no time, no space,
only trees, myriads, upright, vistas and aisles of them
black lacquer gods overlaid with gold leaf,
ancient deities in congregation in the immensity,
half obliterated, forgotten, in the midst of a slow drifting
of flakes of gold.

Again I look in vain for a main verb, but I was interested at that time in making posters with words. As I look over them some of those done from the imagination seem rather good, but these descriptions trouble me with their unfinished air. However, before I leave the notebook I shall catch up a few lines from longer poems because here you have a young writer trying to use the world about her:

The lake is lying flat on its back
and the hills are curled sleepily
propping their heads on their arms—

*   *   *

The long grasses turn up gray-white bellies
like so many minnows dead in a pool.
The splash and drip of everything—it goes to the marrow
it is so cold.

*   *   *

The wet sand and the pools
between the shore and the sand bars
are iridescent like buried Roman glass.

*   *   *

The clouds are torn apart into great windows
that look back into blue phantom gardens:

> *the houses of the clouds are hung with billowing*
> > *black and purple,*
> *passionate palaces.*

How many of us remember the Imagists and the impression they made on young poets? Glancing over some of these poems I can see that I had been reading Amy Lowell and John Gould Fletcher, but here is a simple jingle of Buffalo itself:

> *Indeed I did not know the sky*
> *that roofed our street could seem so high.*
> *I did not guess an elm could be*
> *quite such a stately mystery.*

I could go on, but these samples are surely enough. Who today is really writing Upstate poetry which reflects our countryside? I was making only a first uncertain beginning, and as a more mature writer I seldom returned to Buffalo subjects. But in a notebook begun in July of 1928 I must have been visiting in Buffalo, for I wrote a ballad on the Peddler story of Zoar Valley:

> *In a long valley I have never seen,*
> *they say a river flows between steep hills;*
> *they say the rocks lie smooth among its rills,*
> *they say the woods are very dense and green.*

> *The high shale cliffs are marked by dripping stains,*
> *the few farms have not prospered; one sees deer*
> *standing among the fields, and foxes jeer*
> *the hounds on autumn nights of crying rain.*

> *They say a man goes miles rather than pass*
> *down those steep ruts and by those lonely farms*
> *where at his passing there appear white swarms*
> *of faces clustering behind the glass.*

The people of that valley—so they say—
have each six fingers to a hand, to tell
how once they threw a peddler down a well
and when he clung, struck his two hands away.

They say—they say the curse lies on them still
through generations tilling sour soil,
with furtive eyes and unrewarded toil
in a steep cleft between green hill and hill.

Only once more did I write on a Buffalo theme—or at least a
poem on the Niagara River—and in this case the tragedy and
beauty of the scene have always made me like the poem:

Four years ago a flock of trumpeter swans
flying north, flying proudly along the wind, flying high,
circled down the aërial stairways of the sky,
to that wide river of braided silver and bronze,
Niagara, in the cold water to preen their feathers and rest
with peace in each wild heart and peace in each wild breast.
But fiercer than the winds they knew, fiercer than their
                    hearts flying,
the cold river seized them, the cold river tangled
                    their wings,
the braided river bore them away from familiar things
haughty as dreams and destined like dreams to a
              mythical dying.

THE CATTLE FUNERAL

After the house in Buffalo was sold, my mother and I went to Pasadena alternate winters to visit my Grandmother Reid and Uncle Frank. There was nothing cut and dried about it. We might go abroad for two winters in succession, or to California, but roughly speaking it was a pattern.

During one of these winters we rented for a month a cottage at Palm Springs opposite the small unassuming Desert Inn of those days. Our cottage was of dark redwood, built high, and stood in an orange grove surrounded by a meshed fence like those that enclose military reservations. Beyond us were the thermal springs which still, I think, belonged to the Palm Springs Indians.

Our cottage was owned by a woman doctor who had left with us in the square block of orange trees a Jersey cow, a pinto pony, and the Indian in charge. He was neither young nor old, friendly nor unfriendly to us. Every evening he brought us a quart of the Jersey's milk, which Mother put in a yellow bowl so that she might skim the crust of its cream in the morning. I think he never volunteered a remark, but he answered if we spoke to him.

A little hesitantly in the late afternoon I would ask him to saddle the pinto. I was also a little hesitant about riding a strange horse alone in the desert, for in those days three minutes brought one into the mesquite. A few cattle grazed on tufts of grass here and there—enough, but not too much. The pinto and I followed their winding and tangled trails. The sun was always setting behind us, and the light came across the dark rocky shoulders of

Mount San Jacinto. To the south the range lay in shadow, but to the north the drifted sand dunes burned in changing colors of rose, so beautiful that I could scarcely look at anything else.

You must think of us jogging along at a slow pace, occasionally at a rocking-horse canter, lost in a dream, the pinto as well as I.

There was one afternoon which was the crown of all those enchanted afternoons. I was accustomed to see two or three of the cattle grazing as they could, but on this day twenty or thirty of them had gathered across a shallow dry arroyo from where the pinto and I were passing. They were moving in a slow circle about a dead steer, and as they moved they bellowed, and with their front hoofs threw sand over their lean shoulders, sand which the sunset turned to gold dust. It was a solemn procession, and went on and on with the slow woeful bellowings and the sand thrown first over one shoulder and then over the other.

It was the grief of an older world. So David, hearing of Absalom's death, covered his head with dust; so the mourners of an earlier day followed heroes to their graves, and even today in all primitive parts of the world the hired mourners wail their endless wails.

I cannot remember that the pinto gave the scene a glance, but I watched for a long time and then rode slowly back to the town, while the cattle still circled and cried in their formal and melancholy rites.

Journeys East and West

1914–1929

⋙ At Father's death in 1912 the house in Soldiers Place in Buffalo was sold, and Mother and Margaret and I became homeless and for some years lived in apartments or traveled, though of course I had a four-year harbor at college. It was during the last summer before graduating from Vassar that I joined Mother and Margaret in London, where they had just arrived from Italy. The difference between Margaret's age and mine had always made for occasional friction, but in that summer of 1914 the three years were bridged. We spent most of it on walking trips, while Mother drove in some of the last horse-drawn coaches, complete with horns.

Three important things happened that summer: Margaret and I became life-long friends; I began writing poetry from an inner urge which never left me until eight years ago at Henry's death; and less personally, but more importantly, the first World War began. We happened to be in Stratford the evening before war was declared. The company played Henry V and when the young prince says, "Let us make alliance with the King of France," the entire audience rose to its feet and shouted. Later we were to see the Scots Greys in their kilts marching down the streets of Edinburgh to the skirl of their pipes. People said that you could hear the guns across the Channel. I am not sure that I did but I thought so.

In 1916–1917 came our Wanderjahr, our miraculous adventure in the friendly Far East, a year of which I can only say that it has colored all my life. It had everything in it to excite a young heart and imagination.

In 1919 Margaret married, and Mother and I were footloose for several years. Sometimes we went to Europe, sometimes we spent the winter with her family in Pasadena. When we were abroad we were likely to arrive at Paris. Once we stayed away a whole year, and of that year I remember most vividly Provence in the autumn, Egypt and Sicily, Easter in Spain, and then wild beautiful Brittany. The other trips abroad were less spacious, and are confused in my mind. Oberammergau stands out, and later a trip with a friend through Morocco, of which the memories of Marrakech remain most vivid.

About 1920 we bought the eighteenth-century house called Shipcote in Hingham, Massachusetts, overlooking the harbor, about a mile from the house bought by Margaret and her husband, Morton Smith. At last we had a home, and one which we loved.

But we still traveled, and I still wrote and wrote, and was beginning to publish—my first book of poetry, Fox Footprints, being the direct result of the year in the Orient.

In Britain

◆§ Whether by accident or design I crossed the Atlantic in that summer of 1914 on the same boat as a classmate who was on her way to visit an uncle who was an English vicar in a small village.

I have never forgotten two things that she told me. The first was that her aunt never entered the church, even on a minute's errand, without first putting on her hat; and the second was that her uncle conducted services even if no parishioners were present.

Upon landing in England I was caught in a wind of excitement such as I had not expected. Everything seemed to me so beautiful, and the layers of history back of whatever we saw filled my mind with delight. We began our trip at Tintagel on the coast of Cornwall. It was more than a month later that England declared war on Germany. Most American visitors made the best of their way home in any sort of accommodation they found available. We didn't have the good sense to follow their example. For one thing, the war was very popular in England. On all sides people were declaring "the troops will be home by Christmas." The men we saw taking the trains at the various stations were skylarking, though I can't say that their women, come to see them off, looked so happy. Our chief reason for staying on was that we had not yet seen my Great-aunt Helen Reid in Scotland. Our last visit with her had been in 1898 in Switzerland, where she had gone to be cured of the tuberculosis which had decimated her family.

So we went on, still blind to what was really taking place, still enamored of the world we were seeing for the first time. We sailed home about the middle of September, in time for college, on a small liner which traveled with every light concealed. The sense of danger gave an added zest to the trip. At that time no passenger ships had yet been sunk by submarines. That was to come.

WHEREIN THE BLAME IS LAID UPON
MARK TWAIN

In a deep cove below the ruins of the castle of Tintagel lies a half-moon of shore used now by the fishermen to beach their boats. It was there one black night that Merlin in his windblown cloak stood and watched the waves come from the moaning sea in long lines of phosphorus, till at his feet was laid a child whom he carried secretly to the queen.

The mystery of that sea-birth still hangs over all the bleak stern promontories that face the gray Cornish sea. Few men live along that part of the coast, but here and there lies a weatherbeaten village; or a little church with its ancient baptismal font faces the wind that carries with it all day long the bleating of sheep and the crying of the gulls. On Tintagel Head lie the ruins of the castle where Arthur was raised, a characteristic stronghold of an ancient princeling, three hundred feet sheer above the impotent sea and separated from the mainland by a chasm once crossed by a drawbridge: a fitting eyrie for a sea-eagle who must hold his lands and the respect of his neighbors by his sword.

The sun shone on the rough turf and hardy flowers growing among the rocks. Above the immemorial sea we lay among the broken stones and laughed. For it was not the benign figure of the great wronged king that stood before us, but a squirming Yankee knight whose demoiselle was pouring helmetfuls of water down the neck of his armor to drown a fly, while his good horse looked on in amazement at the hubbub.

THE DUN COW

Ely has its painted angels, Salisbury its spire among the fields, Wells the lovely worn line of its Chapter stairs, York its glass, and high-built Lincoln its peering grotesques, but Durham above the Wear is lovelier than any of them. It is Norman, with a tower instead of spire. The interior has not the delicate arched quality which the Gothic cathedrals retain despite their size, making their naves seem like huge caverns columned with stalactites. In Durham everything is massive, shadowy, stupendous, giving the same impression that one has from mountains and thunderclouds and sullen seas, only this tabernacle to unadorned majesty was a human conception, piled up by human labor.

Nothing could be more masculine than Durham, and its history carries out the impression given by its form. Although the tenth-century bishop who was seeking a resting-place for the bones of Saint Cuthbert was led to the chosen spot by a dun cow, the founder and his successors thenceforth as far as possible ignored the more frivolous sex. A long distance from the altar are two crosses in the pavement, and beyond these no mediaeval woman might put her unworthy foot. The Mother of Christ fared but little better. In other cathedrals it was customary to allot to her the chief chapel directly behind the altar, so that she seemed to sit at one end of the cross with the head of the Crucified in her lap. But Durham would have no Lady Chapel, and discourteously dedicated the position to some male saint.

Fortunately Mary has shown herself without vindictiveness and has demanded no revenge for the slight put upon her and her humbler sisters—unless it was her hand that guided the chisel of the long-dead monk whose statue of the dun cow stands in a carven niche overlooking the square, with what seems to be a most knowing smile.

✂

GRASMERE RECOLLECTION

The view from my bedroom window was bright green from top to sill, cut by the narrow white of a waterfall. At luncheon a butler in purple served cold meats from a sideboard, and the drawing room had two fireplaces, white shelves full of books, and windows across the entire front, looking out on Grasmere and the nursery garden which swept to the water's edge with its roses and phlox.

In the afternoons my mother and sister and I would row past Brothers' Island and its stone shepherd's hut, the bow of our rowboat cutting through a film of sky and cloud while the mountains sunned their friendly crests in a circle about us. This was the land of Wordsworth: here he wandered "lonely as a cloud"— though not half so quietly if the tales of laborers frightened by his wild mutterings be true!—and on the shore near us lay Dove Cottage, where his sister Mary so often read to him until late in the night.

One day on a hillside above the lake I drove off a pair of collies that were frightening the pasturing sheep, and so came to make the acquaintance of the dogs' owners, a middle-aged gentleman and his wife who came up and joined our walk. This pleasant, unnoticeable woman was Wordsworth's granddaughter, born just after his death, and they were returning to the very house the poet had willed to the expected baby if it should prove to be a girl. He himself had built the place and lived in it for a while.

"I often tease my wife about it," said the man, "for the land it's built on used to belong to the village and the old fellow simply appropriated it. He was too big a figure then for anyone to dare question what he did. These dreamers have curious business morals."

Yet it is a picture touched with tenderness, that of the old Wordsworth choosing a spot—even part of the common—for his little house after much consideration and discussion of merits, and finally willing it to the possible girl-baby whom his tired eyes would never see.

GAELIC

From the train windows we had been looking out at hills covered with heather not yet in bloom, their tops lost in the heavy mists so that the streams that came tearing down their sides seemed to come from illimitable distances. Towards dusk we passed a lake and on a point the ruins of a stronghold, romantic as such things are in such a light. It was a castle of the Campbells, and it prompted the little man who shared our second-class carriage to start talking. For he was a Macdonald. First he told of the massacre of Glencoe: of the ride of the old Macdonald chieftain to send in his submission to the Hanoverians; of the fatal holding-back of that document and the coming of the Campbells; of the ten days' feasting and then the murders by night, and the fugitives wandering the hills and dying in the snow. It is an ugly story, and unforgotten. Even today he said, in the Highlands no Campbell picks a spray of white heather for his buttonhole, for the white heather is the Macdonalds' badge.

Then he told us how Crafty Black Duncan of the Campbells was forced to pay for an old sheep's head in a sack, believing it to be the head of an enemy which he had ordered but did not expect to pay for; and why the Macdonalds have a bloody hand on their crest—from the boy who cut off his own hand and threw it on the beach of Skye, when the father offered that island to the son who should first touch its shore. And then he told us of the fairy mounds whose doors open but one night in the year and from which may be heard the sound of little fiddles and bagpipes; and of how the twenty-four Scots witches gathered in a conclave on Mull and, despite the efforts of the Spanish witch, sank the treasure ship of the Armada, which the British government was still trying to raise.

But though he told us the stories he would not talk Gaelic to us; and perhaps it is as well. For we had one memory of the tongue we would not have wished overlaid. It was in a little croft north of Ballachulish, a place with two very small rooms and a loft in which lived a family of six. Only the mother was home, a neat old soul for all her torn dress and broken shoes, and she invited us in out of the rain to sit on creepy-stools in front of a candle-size peat fire while she leaned against the table and entertained us. It was then, to the sound of falling rain and the slight hiss of the peat, that we persuaded her to say the Lord's Prayer in Gaelic. At last she began, intoning the words slowly and reverently and her voice rose and fell, filling the room with an unhurried and outlandish beauty, rough as the furze and singing as the streams that come down the side of the hills.

THE EXILED KWANYIN

We had been walking all morning through the rain towards Ballachulish along a narrow road beside the Caledonia Canal, with the hills partly hidden by the mist rising steeply to our left and the sound of narrow streams falling down their sides continually in our ears. The black-faced sheep with their half-grown lambs were feeding here and there, and once we saw a doe go leaping through the fern; and once we passed a wandering man with a dirty bonnet cocked over his ear, stopping at a cottage door to beg for a match for his pipe. About eleven o'clock we came to a small inn near a ferry, and, wet and tired, stopped to have something to eat. It was an old house—Johnson and Boswell on their tour through the Hebrides had rested there—and it was very simple. The barmaid was in a panic at our entry, the proprietor retired behind his mugs, and it was only after much explanation that we finally found ourselves in a bare room with a peat fire in the fireplace and tea and toast on the table. On the wall was an engraving of a stag, and for other ornaments the place boasted two shells on the mantel, and—I could hardly believe my eyes—a white Kwanyin between them, no prize won at a country fair, but, though broken, of the finest Chinese porcelain.

There she sat, with the veil over her high headdress, throned on lotuses and leaning down towards a little top-knotted child at her feet. In her were all the lovely dreams of Chinese saints and artists who had endowed her with a heart of mercy and put the vase of the water of life in one hand and the branch of willow in the other. We wondered what wandering Scots highlander of another generation had brought the small figure back to his glen, and whether any child had ever mistaken it for that other merciful lady, Mary, with her Babe.

I remember reading in the diary of an English sea captain in the seventeenth century of the shoguns when Christianity was beginning to be proscribed in Japan just before the nation was entirely isolated. Some native women came aboard his ship in one of the ports, and, entering his cabin, shamed him by kneeling and praying in a flood of tears to a "wanton" picture of Venus and Cupid he had upon his walls. It is a moving scene: the little cabin, the kneeling women indifferent to the danger, the captain confused and ashamed, and above them all the smiling casual goddess and her rogue of a son. And yet perhaps a simple conception like that of a child or of those peasant women may have been very near the truth—Venus, Kwanyin, Mary, all are interpretations of love incarnate in a woman.

Indifferent to theology the statue reaches a broken hand down towards the child pressed against her knee.

DOWN HIGH STREET

Old Edinburgh lies on a ridge above the new city, from the castle set superbly on its rock, like a rider curbing an impetuous horse, down the mile-long street to Holyrood. Below is Princes Street, the most beautiful avenue in the world, and all the "crescents" and residence blocks built since Mary used to ride—too forwardly, as many of the Scots thought—clattering down High Street, belled hawk on wrist, or rumbling by in her carriage, bowing that fine thin neck of hers, so white, they say, that through it one could see the purple of the wine she drank.

Along this ridge with its high old houses stands Saint Giles under that crown-tower that looms with so royal a silhouette against the sky. One would never guess that it had once been divided into four churches where four pious and argumentative flocks sat under four different preachers. The upper part of High Street is still respectable, and one recognizes the strong French influence, in a more rugged setting. In the city buildings one may find a statue of Prince Charles Edward in bronze, as a Roman, with a display of lithe jerkined stomach that brought forth the remark from our guide that he "had no got a Scots figure." He also has no true Scots face, but a set of weak silly features that does much to dampen one's instinctive ardor for a lost cause.

Farther down the street, with a bookstore picturesquely occupying the lower floor, is the little house of that arch-hater of Stuarts, John Knox, a man "no willing to juist give and tak," as the same guide said in speaking of him. The most interesting room in the house is perhaps the study, just large enough for a chair and a narrow desk between windows looking out in two directions upon the street—a splendid gallery from which to spy on the evils of his city for material for those thundering sermons. Mary was probably theme enough, going by on her side-saddle, full of her French ways.

And at last, with increasing squalor and perhaps an increasing number of pious mottoes in broad Scots over the doors, we descend to the gates of Holyrood and a cluster of churches and breweries, an epigram in stone on Scottish character. But beyond the palace one climbs the side of Arthur's Seat, lying like a misty green sphinx. The children are trying to fish in the lakes, walking the heather, and overcoming all sorts of hair-raising dangers on the cliffs. And the unshepherded sheep graze and sleep and look out over the silver-gray waves of Edinburgh, tossed below them in long breaking crests, with so distant and serene an air that one wonders whether or not they are just sheep, in this land where True Thomas met the fairies walking like two white harts.

On the Continent

৵§ If man were less adaptable life would be much more vivid.
He would be more often in a state of surprise and not carry with
him a damning capacity for making comfortably commonplace
the experiences into which he falls. Above all perhaps this is true
in traveling. It is always the place one has not seen which gives
the sharpest tang to one's journey. No matter how miraculous a
spot may seem at first glance one feels at home in it after a few
days; the fine bloom of mystery is soon thumb-marked; it is the
next place which hangs like a mirage along the horizon.

There is another aspect of traveling: the breaking of one's
ordinary responsibilities and interests has taken place; letters
follow, but bring only shadows of meaning. A farmer's wife in
Iowa once said to me that when she came back from an auto-
mobile ride, nothing seemed to her worth the doing. She sat idle
with the chickens to feed and supper to get. And traveling is like
that a hundred times over. It is as though one returned to the
early days of the world, every man his own Ulysses making a new
Odyssey.

BORDEAUX

We saw four beautiful things at Bordeaux—all of them eternal or something like it: shipping in a great harbor, two gypsy girls, pigeons sunning themselves on the statues of the cathedrals, and a heavy, primitive farm wagon filled with baskets of grapes covered with colored papers and driven by a young giant astride the shafts. The peasants change little, so do the ways of birds or ships, but the gypsies are especially tenacious of their customs since that curious mediaeval influx of their tribes across Europe. The girls were touched with the East of their origin; they belonged to an unassimilated strain sprung from unknown sources, outcast and wandering for unknown reasons, a curious thread of tarnished tinsel appearing and disappearing through our prosaic present. No one gave these girls more than a cursory glance as they passed, and yet with them went a mystery older than the red stone cathedral with its gilded Virgin.

THE SEA CELTS

The north shore of Brittany is a broken coast of cliffs and rocky islands, and green fields with wild hedgerows, and small villages within smell and sound of the sea. The people are great fishermen, and each year the recruits for the Iceland fleets are drawn from this district to be gone for months in the cold and fogs, out of sight of land. They are a primitive and unspoiled race, almost pagan in their superstitions, and little influenced by the outside world. In many parts they speak only Celtic and think of the French as "foreigners." The type is usually distinctly akin to the Irish with here and there a strong dash of the Spanish among the descendants of the shipwrecked sailors of the Armada, lost in that storm so advantageous to England. They are very religious; their weatherbeaten chapels are filled with votive offerings, especially with the little ships the sailors hang before the altar of the Virgin. And along the roads there are always the stone crosses, often hacked from the earlier Druid menhirs, with a crude but touching figure of the Christ upon one side and of Mary on the other. They dominate the desolate green countryside with a sort of primitive pathos, as though a form had been given to the sound of the sea and of the wind over the gorse.

It is not the sort of country that one would expect to have appealed to a court lady—yet it was here Madame de Sévigné loved to come, all the way from Paris by coach to these wild moors and the little manor she owned, which has with the process of years become a disintegrating farm with rooms rented out to day laborers and their families. We came upon it through the mist, and saw in the courtyard a flock of sheep with their heads all turned timidly towards us, bleating thinly as their hobbles checked their stampede of fear. Hens were roosting on the door, and an old woman took us through the place, so old and so ugly that she seemed like a witch as she scrambled ahead of us crying over and over, "Coz! coz! coz!"—"Old! old! old!" There were stone stairs in a tower with now and then a slab gone, leaving an opening straight into the cellars; the halls were black, we felt our way cautiously; doors opened into rooms where peasants' thick bodies showed black against fires burning in handsome carved fireplaces, and some of the floors seemed to be falling through. All was dirt and decay. And as we looked about us we could not help thinking what a tragedy it would be if some spring morning the fine ghost of Madame de Sévigné should yearn for her beloved Brittany, and she should return, to find this carcass of a manor in uprooted gardens, where she had once lived so exquisitely.

※

LA BRETONNE

At the sea village of Trébeurden, on the wild north coast of Brittany, full of cliffs and rocks sending jagged crests above the water, where the fields are wild and the pasturage thin—"un pays sauvage," as they say—there is a small broken chapel. One pushes open the unlocked door and finds a room like a rough ship's cabin with a Madonna above the sea over the altar; around her are a few offerings of a primitive countryside. This is Notre Dame de Bonnes Nouvelles, a famous chapel in its day.

It was here that Anne of Brittany sent her coronation robes, a long cry from the elegant carved chapels of the Touraine châteaux, or the cathedrals with their towers and spires delicate as icicles. But Anne was not of the stuff that forgets. Gentle Charles called her "Ma Bretonne," or "Bret," and the children

of France still sing of her little wooden shoes. She had grown in
the sea wind; she was a seasoned lover and hater. No one crossed
her with impunity; if her dignity were assailed she could strike
with a cold vindictiveness. She walked with a slight limp which
the courtiers of the day were quick to say made her but the more
graceful, and she ruled her ladies with the stern honesty of a
provincial. Nothing can be imagined greater than the contrast
between her court and the Flying Squadron of her grand-
daughter-in-law, who used the beauty and wit of her maids of
honor to overcome opposition to her plans: but the Italian
Catherine de Médicis had need of whatever intrigue she was
capable of, and was constantly thwarted for all her astuteness.
Anne had no need. No one ever seems to have opposed for long
that indomitable little will. Twice a queen and mother of a
queen, her coat-of-arms of the ermine appears more often on the
walls of the châteaux of the Loire than any other except perhaps the flaming salamander of that great builder, Francis.

THE YOUNGEST SAINT

Opposite where we were sitting the great lancet windows formed
a part of the springing lines of the pillars, and we could scarcely
see the altar of the Virgin in her blue gown on the further side

of the choir, but near at hand through a tangle of ferns we could catch a glimpse of the armored torso of Joan of Arc with her banner pressed against her breast, like a silver page in the court of the Queen of Heaven. It was the day of her canonization, in some sort a crowning of the heroic spirit of France in victory. The church was crowded with people to do her honor. Every rush-bottom chair was filled with a farmer or his wife, a provincial gentleman or his lady, an imp of a child or an old woman in her shawl. The choirboys wandered about casually like straying puppies, and from time to time the verger, an old man, weighted with the finery of the Napoleonic period, cut through the crowd in assisting the public to its seats or ejecting bad boys. Then there was a silence, a craning of necks; the bishop in cloth of gold and purple was moving in full procession towards the altar to celebrate the accession of Joan to the company of saints.

Joan stood ecstatic among the flowers with her banner ("it has borne the brunt, it has earned the honor"), her face turned upwards, as it had been when the bishops crowned the king at Rheims, as it had been that other day when the bishops presided over her burning at Rouen.

THE GARDENS

Like bees to a flower, like buzzards to a corpse, the small boys gather as one draws out one's paints. But the small boys of France are different from those in other places. If one has put in but two or three brilliant meaningless strips of color to place the composition, they murmur to one another, "C'est chic, n'est ce pas?" If the picture is more nearly finished, they will group about it, often standing full in the way, looking for the subject, and ejaculate, "Ah, c'est joli!" They are unconquerably courteous.

The walks of the Luxembourg Gardens on a fine autumn day when the leaves are turning yellow and the flowerbeds are at their height of color, are knotted into strange congestions of people. Nurses with baby carriages, old men, women with broods of children, lovers, and small boys may be seen quietly milling about something hidden, invariably a painter at work. The fountains play gently, adding a fresh coolness to the air, the gardeners with their little brooms sweep the walks, the sun shines warmly on the white statues. No one is in a hurry. All have time to stop, to add their friendliness to the day. It is embarrassing perhaps at the time, many a color is laid on foolishly under the pressure of that ring of eyes, but it is pleasant to look back on later.

There is a little old woman who collects sous, according to French custom, for the rent of the small iron seats of the park. She is neat with that pitiful neatness of the French poor, she is quick as a sparrow. She hops and chirps along the walks from chair to chair, getting a copper here and there to put in her old purse. I was packing my paints as she came up. She stopped to nod her approval (to all of us from tyro to master that smile would be the same) and at my speaking asked if I were English.

"American?" she cried and gave me a quick hug about the shoulders with scrawny little arms. "American? I love the Americans: my two sons are in San Francisco—the only children I have left."

"You will go to them some day?" I asked.

"Oh no!" she said bravely, "I will never see them again"; and then with that little quirk of humor which marks the French courage, "Messieurs les sous will not permit."

And with that she was off again from chair to chair among the flowers, her old black shawl folded closely over her shoulders, and I in turn sauntered down the walks and watched the backs clustered over other people's canvases and sketch-boards, and heard the polite French children murmuring, "Ah, c'est joli, n'est-ce pas?" at other people's efforts, and felt the air from the fountains, and rustled my feet among the sad old leaves that were falling from the branches.

[On the Champs Elysées]

He has the head of a goat and the paunch of Silenus
as he walks down the sidewalks alone, conventionally going
        to dine.
His little bright eyes are glancing, his little hard feet
        are prancing
as though all the crowd about him were maenads and fauns
        in a line.

The horns of the motors for him are puffed by the cheeks
        of centaurs,
the buildings and shops are cliffs, draped and festooned
        with the vine,

and the little cane that he swings he has used on the ribs
     of his donkey
when the ground was rocking with laughter and the trees
     were reeling with wine.

TESTIMONY

Here and there a cemetery, rows and rows of crosses under wind-
torn flags; here and there a village with a few walls, piles of
débris in numbered squares, and a handful of wooden shelters
for the returning inhabitants; here and there a field green or
brown with turned earth through which horses and oxen work
side by side; everywhere else the purple of dry weeds for miles
and miles, dead woods with shattered trunks and tormented
branches; and last of all barbed wire, coiled up by the roadsides,
rusted and fierce.

Our train passed suddenly a group of wooden shacks with
their gardens about them. In one of them there were a few
cosmos in full bloom, and it was with a start of pleasure that I
heard a Frenchwoman say to her husband: "Look! there is the
American flower! Wherever it is growing the Americans have
been!"

THE WORLD OF BRUTES

The fields of Touraine lie along slow rivers, between woods, marked with patches of yellow grain or the green of cabbages. In the stubble the cows feed, with a woman sitting near them, a dog beside her. When they stray too near the vegetables the dog is sent after them; in the meantime the woman knits, usually with her feet straight out in front of her, or nurses her baby, or talks with some friend come out to share the loneliness of the fields. The brightness shines along the cows' ears; they embody the long unthinking afternoons. With them are often those most Gallic of animals, the goats. I have seen two of them driven down a road, rearing and butting as they came; their motions seemed like dancing, the click of their horns was like castanets, and one had a long tendril of grapevine hanging from his mouth. No wonder the ancients, so quick in their appreciations, deified the goat spirits into fauns and Pans!

All day under the chestnuts and poplars go the line of farm wagons, a carter leading the big horses, like elephants in their tasseled ear-coverings and bridles with the dyed sheepskins hanging from the peaks of their collars. Here and there a vegetable cart passes, drawn by a diminutive donkey in full harness, with more leather showing than donkey. Their little feet and rabbit heads have won the tenderness of many French writers, and of that Laurence Sterne who made his sentimental journey among them and is never gentler than when encountering an ass. The dogs, too, are often harnessed to handcarts, and if not jocosely strolling along barking at everything that takes their eyes, seem to throw themselves into their collars with a fury of personal pride. They are very nationalistic too, and the French of a stranger never deceives them into friendliness, unlike the cats who welcome any notice whatever with diplomatic suavity.

These are not perhaps cats unusual for their beauty but they are almost universally mistresses of themselves. By daylight one sees no skulking: they sun themselves among flowerpots, they tuck in their toes on doorsteps, they join the family party about the table. At kitten time they carry on unremitting warfare with the dogs and lie in ambush in the most unexpected places, making canine life uncertain and hazardous.

But this period of strain is temporary. In Touraine the customary mood is peace. Cows, goats, horses, donkeys, dogs and cats—all seem creatures of the sunlight, full-fed and easy, as though they had been created by Summer for her praise.

THE RAGPICKER OF PROVENCE

Streets and roads—how they bind cities and people together! how busily they run through the country! There are some that are arduous and climb hills and drive straight into towns as though their ambition was achieved in turning into thoroughfares. There are some as peaceful as an old priest on a mule, and some, overgrown with weeds, that seem lonely and nursing hurt pride, into which one turns as one chooses a little-used shop surrounded by prosperous neighbors. But large or small, the roads are the meeting places of the people. The statues of the gods used to stand at the crossroads, and today the crosses remind one of Gethsemane, or the Virgins stretch out their hands to the passer-by. The village women coming home from work in the vineyards cross themselves; the men clasp their heads. The roads between the columns of the trunks are still temples.

But in the cities the dignity of the streets is too often lost: everything is crowded, noisy, modern. There are gutters instead of ditches of clear water where the watercress grows; and poverty. The lights of the street lamps are hard with no halo of pity. The shadows move; lean cats creep along the walls; figures pick among the garbage. And yet I have found that one can never be sure of degradation from appearances. One evening I stopped before three patches of white and a daub of darkness bent over an ashcan. With as much politeness as my French was capable of I offered the change in my purse, from that impulse which makes us all at times try to pay toll for our happiness.

And there in the black street, the black figure straightened itself into a woman, and a voice quietly thanked me and refused with all the casual dignity of good breeding.

※

THE CABMAN OF TOULOUSE

A cabman is the especial dispensation of Providence—no one can foresee whether he will be scowling and truculent, plainly intending to force the last sou, or whether he will prove a sort of high priest of his town, extending his pontifical blessing over its streets and showing himself a father to his fares. Such a one was the driver in Toulouse, an old man full of noddings, chucklings, and little hymns of pride and pleasure at each new sight. He showed us the streets, the museum, the great brown Garonne beneath its bridges. Learning that we were Americans, he unbent still further and as an especial favor took us to see St. Sermin and the old houses near it. Before one festooned with garlands and caryatids of stone, he became ecstatic. It was nearly dark, a fact he bewailed, the house was so beautiful. He watched our faces as we looked; he drank in our applause.

Unwillingly at last he snapped his great whip like a thunderclap, startling everyone but the horse; yet halfway down the next street he could no longer contain his feelings. He pulled up his horse again. He ordered me by a single magnificent gesture to stand up so that I might not miss a word. He was quivering with excitement: "That house is the most beautiful in all the world," he confided. "Neither in England nor in Italy nor in America nor even in the rest of France is there a house to be compared with it." Then, and only then, like the ancient mariner was he satisfied to have expressed himself; and like the wedding guest I sank back released from his glittering eye. The old horse broke into an unwilling trot, and we jolted back through the settling darkness to our hotel.

TULIPS

No wonder the tulip is the patron flower of Holland. Looking at it one almost smells fresh paint laid on in generous brilliance: doors, blinds, whole houses, canal boats, pails, farm wagons— all painted in greens, blues, reds, pinks, yellows. The vision rises of the little houses, like tulips in rows, the boats in the harbors in rows, the pollarded trees in rows, and the wooden shoes in rows before the door. And the texture of the flowers is almost as starched as the white headdresses of the women, as swelling as their skirts and copper jugs.

But with all this domestic gaiety and freshness there is in the tulip something exotic, a parrot flare, a suggestion of the tropics and brown rivers. There is a refusal to seek shelter among its leaves, preferring to meet the wind upright or be snapped completely, recalling the heavy hearty men of Holland's great period, soldier-admirals in their broad-thighed vessels holding the sovereignty of the seas, exploring the remote corners of the earth and giving place to no one.

DUTCH ARCHITECTURE

From the walls of the museum in Haarlem the portraits of Frans Hals looked down, slyly masterful, far more living than the wizened old men that moved beneath them. But behind their dynamic presence the shape of the rooms asserted itself in an unconquerable serenity. The building had been a house of the fifteenth century, with simple spacious proportions. It was difficult to realize that it had been a contemporary of those narrow burghers' dwellings, climbing story above story into a jumble of sharp roofs and dormers, that leaned over nearly every street in Christendom. This house had far more in common with the Japanese than with the Gothic. There is the same sense of proportion and of restfulness and leisure, the same simplicity.

And among European nations it was Holland who first appreciated the possibilities of landscape art, and of animals and birds and still-life, which China and Japan had so long and so beautifully recognized. It is true that the Dutch approached the subjects from a different angle, with a robust earthliness that differed widely from the mysticism of the Orient. But the important fact is that both *did* approach them. There was some inexplicable affinity of spirit they shared. And in later times when a contact had been established between the two nations it is extremely interesting to recognize the profound influence upon Dutch artists of the Japanese prints that filtered through Europe from the trading station on the island off Nagasaki, where Holland, alone of the West, was permitted a limited intercourse with the hermit kingdom—which was itself influenced by the few Dutch paintings that came its way.

THE RETURN TO ANDERSEN

In coming into the mountains everything conspired to turn time back to my childhood. The heights on either side might have been those on which Heidi kept her grandfather's goats, and the door of the hotel at Geneva was opened by a Swiss doll I had loved as a little girl. I faced her for some time with the amazed sense of having known her before. And then there is the Island of Rousseau in the middle of the river that pours out from Lake Geneva, glass green and boiling into smooth springs that reflect the clouds. From it I saw eight swans flying past—the seven brothers and their sister, the children of a king, all with a strong beating of white wings, and their long throats reaching out towards the sunlit mountains beyond the city. I knew it was a royal vision, and the air stirred by their haughty wings was the clear air of fairyland.

LA GLOIRE

Lamartine sat all one day under a tree beside a dusty roadside by Lake Geneva. And at last they passed, Mme. Récamier and Mme. de Staël. "Hélas! comme tout le monde," wrote he charmingly, "je n'ai saisi ma vision qu'au vol, et je n'ai vu l'amour et la gloire qu' à travers d'un grand chemin."

Madame de Staël's little château to which they were driving that immortal day stands back in a grove of trees above the village of Coppet. There is a stream and a waterfall beside the walk, and terraces in front, looking down towards the lake. It was here that she held court with the twig of green leaves in her hand placed fresh every morning beside her breakfast plate, suggesting —who knows?—the laurel with which "Corinne" was almost visibly crowned.

Her presence fills the house, an untidy, heavy-mouthed eager sort of woman with black curls escaping from an oriental turban, to judge by the portraits that still hang on the walls. She was a storm of a creature and talked till even her cultivated guests longed for the relaxation of some less intense and intellectual an atmosphere. Byron used to walk on these lawns with her; it was here, too, that parts of her tempestuous love affairs took place. And here came her friend, Mme. Récamier, and lived in a bedroom with Chinese wallpaper of plants and birds, a lovely setting for her loveliness. The most brilliant and the most beautiful women of their time under one roof—it is no wonder that the young romantic Lamartine sat by the roadside, or that we return to Coppet to catch a glimpse of their figures, hidden not by the dust of the highway, but of years.

On the Mediterranean

🖋 Around the shores of the Mediterranean every race has left its mark in stone and in flesh: the women of Arles are as Greek as the temples of Sicily; the Berbers gather olives from trees planted, it is said, by the Romans; the Spanish Jew, seeking Turkish protection, has for four hundred years spoken Castilian in the streets of Constantinople. Yet it is not blood altogether that decides whether a man shall kneel on a carpet facing Mecca, or say the Ave Maria before the shrine of the Virgin. Old elements of race and tradition are eternally recombining, and nothing happens in any part of the Mediterranean which does not affect the whole.

SPAIN

Other countries have done far more for the world than Spain: not from her came the Renaissance, nor the great poets, nor science, nor invention, nor philosophy. What she has done has seldom been constructive; she has not built up her nation slowly and painfully. One sees her outlined against banners, against sails, drunk with conquest and tinged with madness. With her loss of rule everything was lost but pride. Of all European nations she alone belongs to the vanished youth of the world. Behind her seas and mountains she lies in romantic isolation, remaining always to the imagination of her neighbors alien and romantic, an Eastern nation at heart.

Spain is, above all else, Catholic Spain. All her history has been spent in fighting the enemies of her religion—Moslem, Jew, or Reformer—and the belief that only death could atone for nonconformity was bred into the bone. Goya, who painted the court, also produced a series of sketches of the Inquisition and of the Napoleonic invasion which for their horror have never been surpassed. As Havelock Ellis has said, there is something closely akin to the savage in the Spanish temperament: its violence, indifference to pain, its laziness (the beggar, not the laborer, is proud), its capacity for bursts of terrific energy, its endurance, its courage, pride, and love of all that is ceremonial. De Amicis wrote of one of Goya's riot scenes, The Third of May: "It is the last point which painting can reach before being translated into action; having passed that point one throws away the brush and seizes the dagger—after those colors comes blood."

There are also at the Prado many pictures of the older Spanish painters: the dark dramatically religious paintings of Ribera; the realism of Zurbaran; El Greco's pale sharp colors and shattered lines; and the gray distinction of Velasquez. In art, as in all else, Spain has been a land of great individual personalities.

[Towards Granada]

There is not a horse in the cavalcade that is not dancing.
They are Christian horses, they know they will be stabled
        tonight in Moslem stalls,
their hoofs shall strike fire from the streets of Granada,
the bell-like jingling of their bits mingles
        with the chanting of the priests,
their whinnying is shrill as triumphant trumpets,
and their cavalcade is a dance of triumph beside the waters
        of La Vega.

Leading them all, side by side, go the two horses
        of Ferdinand and Isabella
in trappings of jeweled velvet. Beautiful wide nostrils
        flare on a line with beautiful nostrils,
thin pricked ears with pricked ears, smooth-moving shoulder
        with shoulder—
knee to knee the Catholic sovereigns ride to take over
        the keys of Granada,
to cleanse their splendid Spain of the last black blood
        of the infidels.

The faces of royalty are masks of triumph, but the horse
        of Ferdinand is fidgeting:
he feels a prickle of spurs but is drawn back
        by the discipline of the curb.
The king looks sideways at the queen and there is dislike
        and entreaty in that look
but she will not meet it. Her hands lie quiet on the reins and
        her horse keeps easy pace with his.

The king looks questingly and freely over his shoulder
            at the queen's ladies.
God in His heaven!—some glance has answered his!
He smirks. His horse gives a little bound under him.
For an instant Isabella's horse falters at the tightening
            of reins in her convulsed hands,
then regains his place. Oh, if she will hold him back
a foot—six inches—how delightfully the king
            will smile at her,
how tenderly he will look at her, how entirely he
            will be hers:
let the nose of her horse be but even with the shoulder of his
            and she will have won for herself a loving husband.

The horses of the Christians are dancing beside
            the waters of La Vega.
They are remembering how it feels to tread down
            Moslem bodies,
they are imagining their teeth again in Moslem horseflesh,
they are thoroughly enjoying the sensations of conquest.
But the horses of Ferdinand and Isabella pace soberly,
            sedately, step matching step.
A queen may break her heart indeed, but Castile
            shall never be humbled by Aragon.
In masks of triumph, side by side, the Catholic sovereigns
            ride beside La Vega
to take possession of Granada.

THE THRONE OF ITALY

Everywhere the magnificent matter-of-fact work of the Roman Empire has been changed into something melancholy, primeval, and strangely beautiful. Not even modern Rome destroys this effect, and certainly not the mediaeval Rome of the popes. There are the villas filled with paintings, among their statued gardens overlooking the city; there are the beautiful massive fountains spouting thick streams of water or pyramids of spray down the wet sides of marble allegories; there are the bridges and the churches (so often ugly), and last the Vatican with the colossal mass of St. Peter's to one side, and to the other—a little further off—the Castel del S. Angelo, once Hadrian's tomb, and later a convenient shelter for popes in times of disturbance, with dungeons always at the service of the popes' enemies. There is nothing in these buildings that breaks away from the heavy, ponderous circles and arches of the old ruins.

One may not be fond of St. Peter's but one must admit that it has dignity—as well it might, having had its share in costing Catholicism the support of all the northern countries of Europe. Here the pageantry of the mediaeval church reached its most fantastic heights in the days of Farnese, who was nearly hanged for forgery before he became pope, or of Borgia, to whose son Cesare was dedicated Machiavelli's *Prince*, and whose daughter Lucrezia sometimes sat on the throne of the popes and received envoys in her father's place, to the scandal of Christendom. Thanks to the taste of just such popes the great collections of the Vatican were accumulated; thanks to them Michelangelo was hauled back more than once against his will to work on The Last Judgment and the ceiling of the Sistine. Here are the Apartments and the Stanze which the facile Raphael painted—that beautiful young man, the grace of whose pictures pleased the taste of the time so completely that Michelangelo was almost forgotten. They tell how, dressed in silks and velvets, riding among the young nobles, he passed the old broken-nosed Titan stumbling back to his dark room where perhaps he and his apprentices were sleeping four in a bed.

THE SWAN'S NEST

Venice the city is stranded like a wrecked galley, rotting but beautiful, and has been ever since the discovery of the Americas when the sea routes to Asia left it only a provincial harbor on an inland ocean. It was a Venetian, Marco Polo, who as early as the thirteenth century sowed the seeds for the ruin of Venice when he adventured into China. It was his matter-of-fact trader's chronicle that helped to arouse the curiosity and greed of Europe which would culminate centuries later in the circumnavigation of the globe. At a time when the unknown East was truly a country of fables to the imagination of Europe, Marco Polo crosssed the entire continent of Asia, estimating populations, customs, religions, exports and imports with surprising restraint and regard for truth. He penetrated the court of Kublai Khan, where he became a trusted councillor, and years later returned to Venice loaded with riches and honors. His story sounds like a fairy tale. But more remarkable still, after seven centuries, he is held in honor in China. Go to the Temple of the Five Hundred Ahrats or Wise Men in Canton, and there—mustachioed, in a grotesque imitation of mediaeval Venetian costume—seated among four hundred and ninety-nine Oriental sages, sits the image of Marco Polo at this minute, with joss-sticks burning before him.

TUNIS

"The white burnoose of the prophet" the Mohammedans call Tunis. It is a true city of the moon—not the French Quarter of course, but the old Arab city of white-walled houses and courts. The men often wear a flower over one ear. Their lemon-yellow slippers hardly make a sound. Their robes are all of soft pigeon-breast colors, or white, or pale blue. The women of the lower classes wear heavy black veils wound about their faces, leaving a slit for the eyes, except the Jewesses, enormously fat, who go with uncovered faces, and are swathed in pure white like Roman matrons.

No unbeliever may enter the mosques of Tunis. One sees only their domes like large moons settling among the flat roofs. Their towers are square and patterned with bricks like the famous Giralda in Seville. Many of the inhabitants are descended from Andalusian refugees, and still keep old deeds and rusted iron keys to houses in Spain that belonged to their ancestors.

These men, they say, are especially to be found among the merchants in the perfume souk. Of all the souks, that of the perfumes is the most beautiful. The red and green pillars that support the numberless low domes of the arcade are supposed to have come from Carthage. The people pass like ghosts, and the air is stirred by a faint odor of incense. The other sections include the rows of shoemakers, cross-legged, pounding and stitching soft leather; there are the merchants of cloth, and of embroideries, and the sellers of weapons, and the saddlemakers. Several times during the day boys bring trays of small cups filled with strong coffee and all the merchants and their customers drink. In the shadowed whiteness everything seems enchanted like the inside of the moon, and one can quite understand the feelings of the holy man who ordered his tomb to be made in one of the bazaars where he might always hear the *slip-slip* of passing feet above his head.

Not many miles across the bay are the remains of Carthage, that city of merchant princes, so treacherously betrayed by Rome.

The height of the old citadel is crowned now by the Trappist monastery where the silent monks work and meditate. Most of the ruins that remain are Roman. Only the Punic harbors are still there, two shrunken pools beside the blue African sea. A few miles to the west is Cape Carthage and the town of Sidi-ben-Saïd, with its mosque raised to Saint Louis, who died here on his last crusade, tending his plague-stricken soldiers. The Mohammedans venerate him as a holy man, and indeed believe that he was converted to their religion on his deathbed. A little farther out in this blue sea lay for many centuries the treasure galley sunk in some storm off the coast as it was sailing from Greece to Rome. Today its freight of bronze and marble is to be seen in the Bardo, the palace of that powerless figurehead of the French, the Bey.

As one stares out to sea, lying in the grass among the poppies, the fishing fleets begin to round Cape Carthage returning to port. Their sails, sharp as the fins of sharks, seem racing on some unknown chase. They make one remember the tales of Barbary pirates, of raids along the coast as far north even as England, of a whole mad romantic nightmare not brought to an end until in the early nineteenth century the Dey of Algiers so far forgot himself as to strike the representative of France with his fan, and by that *coup d'éventail* brought upon himself the destruction of his pirate empire.

And behind all this coast lie the great wheat fields that once fed Rome with the African tribute of grain. Now the great farms belong to the French or English, but the yellow aqueducts of Rome stride across the plains, and the ragged shepherds feed their flocks under olive trees planted by the Romans. Their towns are left in the hills—theatres, temples, forums, and houses, in many of which the Bedouins now live, roofing over old walls, treading daily on mosaiced floors. Only today it is France that rules the people of northern Africa. As we walked down the old pavings of Dougga, marked deep with Roman chariot wheels, we saw ahead of us an Arab striding silently, followed by a woman with her face smeared with tears, and her body jerking with sobs.

"It is the day of the lottery," said a man near us; "her son has been taken for the French army."

Just so must the alien Romans have recruited their African legions for fighting on distant frontiers.

UP THE RIVER

On the journey up the Nile day after day the boat sailed near enough to the shore for us, my mother and me, to watch everything that went on. The people live very close to the animals and all the beasts seem to understand what is said to them. But there is the proverb "God made the Egyptians, and then he made a big stick," and no one seems so happy as when he has authority to hit something. It may be an overseer at the excavations tapping the back of each of the hurrying children as he or she runs past with a load; it may be a policeman with his heavy cane; it may be the dragoman striking out at the donkey-boys who are crowding too close; or it may be these same boys laying on to their animals—but in every case the stick is wielded with an air of peculiar satisfaction.

This latent savagery among a people usually so docile and gentle we did not think of very often under that monumental sky. There are the ruins of great Heliopolis, City of the Sun; there is Sakkara, where a little sphinx sits over a sparrow-haunted pool; there are the remains of Bubastis, where the cats were worshipped; and the great temples of Abydos, where the people hate foreigners, but the temple walls are covered with the loveliest reliefs of the prettiest of goddesses and the brightest of heaped-up offerings. Most of the trips from our steamer we took on donkey-back, a scamper of half a dozen miles each way, with the donkeys racing one another, and a native guard on a camel trying to keep ahead, and the dragoman calling out, "Galloping donkeys not allowed," and everyone laughing, and some beast stumbling and throwing its rider, and the peasants driving their flocks out of the way, and a comfortable awareness in everyone's mind of the tea that will be waiting on the cool decks of the Nile steamer; and then suddenly all else wiped out before the presence of some vast temple, like a hollowed mountain for size, its great walls carved in low relief with smooth and subtle figures.

At Assuan the boats stop, for there the cataract comes rushing down past rocks ground smooth and shining as the backs of huge wet animals, and one must change steamers if one is to go further. The village is full of rough bazaars, where they sell leatherwork and the famous scarves of net and silver. Above the cataract in the lake formed by the dam built by the British to control the Nile, are the temples of Philae, standing like islands half submerged in the water. Here at the first cataract started many of the old trade routes, dangerous, insecure, but connecting Egypt with the lands of the East.

On the way out to the quarries we came upon an encampment of the desert people. The men stayed near the coarse camels'-hair tents, but the women and children crowded about us. They had large bright eyes, and their hair was plaited in innumerable small plaits. They were dark, fine-featured, aquiline like the profiles on the temple walls, and the young girls ran easily as animals. It is said that they can travel four days through the desert with no other food than a handful of seeds, and year by year, probably without break from the time of the Pharaohs, they come from the Red Sea to trade with the Egyptians, following the old caravan route from the land of Punt.

THE HOLY CITY

On an early January day nothing can be imagined more desolate than Jerusalem. A cold wind blows, taking one's breath away. It is probably raining mercilessly. The grass among the stones and painfully terraced hillsides is dead. The city rises on a rocky hill, like a rock-pile itself, dominated bleakly by foreign hospices and churches. The Mount of Olives is crowned by the German Hospice, where the Kaiser and Kaiserin are mosaiced on the ceiling in the guise of Byzantine monarchs. The spot where the Lord's Prayer was first said is covered by a convent of French nuns. The five domes of the Russian Hospice rise above the Garden of Gethsemane. And off in the hills the little town of Bethlehem is ugly with modern missions and orphan asylums. There is not a holy place in Jerusalem that is not marked by some appropriating building. At first the life of the city seems almost commemorated out of existence.

But as the days go by one begins to lose this first impression and to feel through driving rains and tearing winds the charm of the city. The real power of Jerusalem over one's mind lies in a sense of its spiritual significance. It is this fervor of many races, this age-long spiritual intensity, that turns Jerusalem— mosques, synagogues, churches, old town and new town—all into one hill of prayer.

In the East That Lies West

◆§ It is a pity that America, big as she is, has so little room for pilgrimages. If there is one thing better than others, it is a pilgrimage. It is a travel often undertaken by whole families, with homely preparations, councils, expectations. It has a strong dash of adventure, too. And then, it is serious: there is a light of tapers about it, angels fan their wings in the smoke of the train, God bends from above, smiling to see one's sins lightened. The place is almost always beautiful, as miracles very properly occur most often on heights or in the heart of mountains or in woods, and man has done what he could to show his respect and appreciation. Then there is at the spot the combined effect of a fair and a church: there are shops where one may buy candles, offerings, or religious souvenirs; there are also shops for postcards, wine, and dinner. One goes into a chapel to pray and burns with a white light of aspiration: one comes out and looks at the view, runs across a friend, gossips, drinks wine, and returns to pray. Purgatory is less dark, and earth also. In short it has been an occasion, and there are too few in life. The church, which may or may not deserve it, is perhaps a bit richer for one's offering, but usually the price is not dear for the return in eased conscience and the jog to one's interest in life.

The churches of miracles in France, at Lourdes or on the heights of Lyons, the sacred grottos and crypts take back one's mind to the holy spots of the Orient. Nothing in Japan I think is supremely beautiful without being also sacred. Fujiyama for example is a place to which pilgrims are sent from all over the country, whole villages clubbing together to pay the expenses of their representative, expenses which, though relatively small, must loom large in the eyes of poor peasants.

I remember how the sandaled feet kept pattering over the long crooked bridge that leads out to the Island of Enoshima with its caves and goddesses black with brine; how the shadow of drinking pilgrims fell on the shoji of the crowded inns of Miyajima; the clapping of hands all day long before the painted temples in the cryptomeria groves of Nikko; and perhaps particularly the jolly crowd of farmers come to see the sacred girdle that binds together the rocks of Futami. It was towards the end of the season for planting rice and as his fields were finished each small cultivator of the countryside brought his household, and the farm men and girls who had been stooping for days from dawn until dark over the rice shoots, looking in their big hats like toadstools growing from the brown water in which they worked. Now they were having their reward in the pilgrimage, a small one it is true, but there were the booths with the cheap toys and boxes on boxes of shells; there were the minute inns where one might have sake in the shade if the afternoon was hot; there were the sacred rocks before which to pray, and the great bright sea which they seldom saw. The children's slant eyes were full of excitement as they pulled at their fathers' hands; the wives clattered by happily with umbrellas over their heads; the farm boys and girls were laughing and nudging After seeing the grueling work of the planting it was decidedly a pretty thing to see this peasant pilgrimage.

Only the new countries pay for their cynicism by a sacrifice of much of the charm and simplicity of life.

THE OLD WOMAN OF
AMANO-HASHIDATE

"Why is she cursing at us?" we asked as the old woman stood by the side of the road calling out angrily.

"She is not," answered the Japanese friend who spoke English. "She is scolding the boys for not calling out sooner. As it was, she didn't hear anything until so late that she delayed you while getting her handcart out of the way, and now she is afraid the honored foreigners will think that the people of her village are without courtesy."

O grim, stately brocaded past of Japan! When the samurai knelt with smiling lacquered face, receiving the daimio's order to kill his own son with the swords whose silver-patterned hilts were thrust into his belt; when the philosopher drank tea ceremonially before the kakemono in the alcove; when the lady tied her knees together with her butterfly obi and, writing a matchless small poem of farewell, cut her throat before the family altar so that no love for her might lay its hand on the sword-arm of her young husband going forth in a hopeless cause; when the merchant, denied all political outlet, patronized the arts, and cultivated iris in his pools, and bought the color prints of Kyonobu or Hakusai to keep a draught from the kitchen lantern; when the peasant, planting rice in his terraces, bowed his sun-shielded head to the ground, like a mushroom broken in the wind, at the passing of his lord's palanquin, and answered his questions if called upon with an exact deference, any slightest slip in which might cost him life itself.

Beautiful, stern composure of old Japan, sword-taught and delicate, your intricate pattern is wearing thin and breaking beneath the push of Western thought and custom. The shoguns have passed to their glorious tombs among the hills of Nikko, and with them the soul of the samurai. Only on the stage shall we see that passion never shattering through its patterned mold of calm; find the simple exaggerated courtesy only in old people along little-used roads, where the small broken stone Jizos, like elves dressed as priests, guard the field corners.

Our kuruma boys laughed at the outland interruption, and the pad pad of their sandaled feet on the road that Hiroshige once walked was like the hurrying of years.

THE SEA LANTERNS

In front of the little fishing village stretches out a great, almost landlocked, bay, scattered with little islands whose cliffs are fluted by the water to hollows like great shells, above which grow pine trees twisted in the sea wind. Some have steps fashioned from the rock down to the water's edge and man-wrought caves set with images of stone with many arms and fantastic headdresses. But except for the gods these islands have no inhabitants, save one long stretch of land across the mouth of the bay on which is a miserable village and several inns.

It is the custom for strangers to hire a fishing boat to this outer island where there is a sandy beach and water free of all floating seaweed. Here the Japanese girls wade and splash in their under-kimonos and red underskirts with blue and white handkerchiefs on their heads, while the men, dropping their robes among the shells, throw themselves naked into the cold assault of the waves, figures of bronze amid the rush of the incoming sea.

Once a year a ceremony is held for the souls of drowned fishermen, whose bodies lie unburied in the ocean vastness. Perhaps some evening when the moonlight shines indistinctly on the seaweed of the bay, a host of lanterns, yellow and red, set upon little rafts of straw, is put adrift in a great circle on the still surface. It is like a ring of gnomish sails that move gently to and fro as the currents carry them. Some slowly make seaward, others turn towards the land. As though drawn by invisible hands they drift under the moon, past the scattered islands and their stone gods. In an hour only two or three lanterns are still to be seen, answering with their flickering brilliance the round glow of the moon. The drowned sink back to the long sway of the seaweeds and the green of the under-ocean, satisfied now that the annual reverence has been paid them.

By morning the shore is strewn with a wreckage of straw and sodden paper, a broken garland returned from the presence of the dead.

THE FOX-WOMAN

She was the first to speak: "You are right, I am a fox-woman.
These silk kimonos and brocaded obis, this hair like a wig of
lacquer, and these geta with their red thongs passing between
my toes—they are all so much enchantment, so much mummery
to amuse myself when the moon shines along the water of the
rice terraces and I hear the sound of singing and the playing of
the koto that comes up from the villages like smoke blown from
a fire. Then I grow tired running in the moon with my nose
tipped with flame; I grow tired carrying through the fields the
messages of Inari and calling songs to the moon, and a loneliness
comes upon me in the midst of my companions. It was not to
lure your soul to destruction that I created this little house by
the roadside, and threw the image of a beautiful face across the
shoji that you might see it in passing. Look, there on the shelf
stands the image of the Buddha, with the light of my lantern
on his face. It is true that he is but an appearance, yet all the
universe is but an appearance, and he is as real as the solemn
statues that sit in the temples year after year with the doves
cooing among the eaves. On nights like this I pray to him with
my forehead on the matting, saying, 'O Buddha made by a fox,
have pity upon a fox.' Under his benediction you are safe. And I
have even remembered to create a cricket in a little cage of
wicker that he may sing as we talk. Of what are you afraid? Of
the loneliness in the heart of the fox, or of the beauty with
which she has clothed herself on this spring evening? You would
not be afraid if you saw me running along the ground with the

dew wet on my fur, and the stars shining in my eyes. And here you shall sit upon mats that will be none the less soft because they are not true mats, and you shall see me dance more beautifully than any dancer you have ever seen, so that the only sound will be the rustle of my skirts and the deep intake of your breathing; and you shall have sake from cups of white jade, like those from which the seven sages of China drank long ages ago when they left the courts to live in the mountains far, far from the dense shapes of reality. Of what are you afraid? I will sing you songs of the old days of the gods and you will see the moonlight fall through the shoji in blue fragrance upon the yellow heart of this little room, and incense will rise to your nostrils bringing with it dreams, and you will forget that I am a fox, and think that I am an empress who has come to you from the grave with soft words and sighings. My hair is blue-black and heavier than a fringe of the thickest silk, and my eyes are like lacquer set in ivory, and my body is a willow tree swaying in the south wind. We are all visions dreamed by the gods, as they sleep. If I am a vision of a single evening, and you perhaps of seventy years, am I the less lovely for that? Do not leave me, for even a fox can be grateful, and my heart is estranged from the moor and the wind and it yearns after the comfort of human intercourse and human laughter and praise."

◈§ Of all the countries through which we traveled during those marvelous thirteen months, I loved China the most. At that time it was half ruinous, with the especial sadness and poetry that hang like a mist over ruins; I doubt if I should care much for communist China, though it may be a better place to live in. There were many books on China and Chinese poetry which I got hold of, none of them very good translations from the Chinese—Arthur Waley's work was still to reach us—but I could transform the pedestrian translations in my mind.

I think my whole preference for China could be epitomized by a flaking wall near a temple, on which someone had sketched a narcissus and a line of Chinese characters. In Japan that would soon have been tidied up. But not in China, the lovely decrepit China of those days.

𝕏

SILVER PAPER

We followed the spring into China—it was early spring in the botanical gardens at Hong Kong, the smell of it was in the air. It was spring from the Peak. The fishing craft in the intricate islanded harbor below seemed like butterflies tilting on blue silk. Through all the dust and cold Shanghai was quivering with April; the peach blossoms showed through the fruit-patterned lattices of hidden gardens; willow branches were hung over the gateways; the crows wheeled in loud circles, and the little tile figures on the curving eaves rode boldly against a dappled sky.

We had the tingling heavy waywardness of spring on the Grand Canal, in the red comely cheeks of the boatwomen swinging at the oars, smiling, shouting orders to their children while the hens squawked in their wicker cages overhanging the poop. The masts of the fishing junks with their scarlet pennons seemed like the patterning of spears of an army led to a campaign against the sea. From their bows the painted eyes of the junks peered at us across the water. Everything was magnified and potent. The mustard fields were in flower, such wicked sulphurous bloom in flat land through which ribbed sails moved slowly along unseen canals. The yellow was like an emanation from the graves with which the country was filled, houses of tile built about a coffin, sometimes broken to show a white skull among a clutter of bones, gazing up at a blank sky.

Once we saw along a towpath, outlined against clouds, a beggar in fluttering blue rags leading a black bear on a chain, both with their heads down against the rain, wanderers through these villages whose gray curving bridges and canal-built houses made them seem like squalid Venices. Once we passed a shrine roofed with orange straw and overhung by an immense tree with every limb cut off except one in which was wedged the black blotch of a rooks' nest. The hens were sheltering under the dwarfish mulberry trees, the ducks quacking about the ricks; and I remember between showers a boy at a farm flying a swallow-shaped kite that fluttered its curving wings and long tail in a darting struggle against the string that held it.

And West Lake was in a dream of springtime, a haze from the faint emerald mountains to its shallow sheet of water crossed by causeways like threads with arched bridges on which the passing buffalo looked like figures on a tusk in some cabinet. And like a bubble formed on the dreaming lake was the island where the causeways met.

And it was still spring that ran northward before us like a crier to Peking, and shook down the heavy blossoms over the bronze phoenix in the court of the summer palace; that made the women in the coolie kitchens smile like Holbein women in the yellow dusk behind the brass pots, and set one girl to embroidering in the sunlight of her door, her baby in a basket at her side, and on her knee a tiny pot of artificial flowers from which she copied. It put fire in the haughty blood of the hawks they sold at the temple fair; it tossed petals into the pools to deceive the goggle-eyed goldfish.

And still spring called us north through the sandstorms and taught the brown larks to sing in their cages hung before each door in the bleak streets of Kalgan, until the dust was vibrant and the grotesque camel trains of the Mongols strode through lanes of singing. Within the flamingo-colored courtyards of the

Ming tombs in the ruined valley sprang up the scentless purple violets and the wild fleur-de-lis from whose roots the women make white powder for their faces. But the burnt-gold mountains and the Wall that rides their slopes and abysses neither the seasons nor the centuries may touch. And there we lost our long-followed spring forever, with its mists and sands and birds and the blossoms for whose passing souls the Chinese women once burned silver paper in the temple braziers.

CANTON

To everyone his own China. Mine is an emotion, a fused sense of mystery and age, of splendor and delicacy and decay, of horror and beauty. Into it go all the suggestions of the past, the old Cathay that lay shadowed by dragons at the end of the earth, the caravan routes from Persia; the fierce conquests from the north; poets painting on silk held by court ladies in summer-houses over lotus lakes; dreamers among the crags of mountains; armies marching through the heavy dust; dynasties crashing to ruin among burning palaces; and the tall trading ships of the West bartering for tea and porcelains, and filling the ports with their swaggering pigtailed sailors.

And with all the sense of the past there is the present, which seems scarcely more real. Looking back I realize how close the relationship is between ideas and things: the China that we saw was a continuation, a part, of the China we had only thought about. There was greater grandeur to the north, it had the desolation and starkness of centuries. One can never forget the sight of the walled cities across the sands, with the dunes sweeping in a long inevitable line almost to the tops of the city walls, or the stricken peace of the Valley of the Ming Tombs. It is on the Yangtze that the fleets of junks are most majestic, and West Lake is like a dream that has turned to water.

And yet in the final impression of China one's mind goes back to the south, to that race of insurrectionists and rebels, those small seething people of Canton. It too is a city with a wall, but one that never impresses the onlooker as do those in the north.

There are many interesting things in Canton, the old water-clock on the street of bookstores; the Flowery Pagoda with its nine roofs; the Mohammedan Pagoda near the river, which was the first thing the Arabian merchants saw as they drew near the city in the tenth century; the Five Fairies' Temple with its stone sheep; the building where the coffins wait with their paper attendants till an auspicious burying-place is discovered.

Yet the real Canton is never caught in any building, unless the whole city be considered as one, so narrow and winding are its streets, thin clefts, a web of arcades above which one sometimes sees a roof of matting. The stores open their interiors wide by day, the shutters stacked away, and above on the shelves the gods sit with blue incense curling before them. In time of riot heavy gates close one district of the city from another. It is in these dark, tortuous, sinister and charming streets that one feels Canton. There are whole districts of silk stores, or of apothecaries; even more fascinating, streets of bookstores or porcelain, lacquer or jewelry. I remember one crazy four-story building at a corner, with a tumbling room on each floor, filled with wallpaper strips painted with the most delightful birds and flowers, elegant and joyous, like the wallpapers that were brought from China in the eighteenth century and which one sometimes sees in the French châteaux.

There are seventy-two guilds in Canton, beginning with the bankers and ending with the weavers, and running through such fascinating and unexpected guilds as those of the bean-curd makers and signboard painters, of the dealers in kerosene lamps and in articles made of pear-tree wood, and of the dealers in gold thread used in embroidery. I feel less friendly towards the guilds of fishmongers and fresh-fish merchants. Too often have I walked on their bloody pavements, and seen them tie a string neatly about the middle of a fish dipped from a pail, and hang it on a customer's finger while it gasped like a surprised alderman about to pour forth a torrent of abuse.

More than in any other place I have ever been, even Chicago, one receives from Canton the sense of life, of hurry, of endless vitality. The clerks sit in their open shrine-like stores, sometimes as motionless as the gods above them on the god-shelf, but everyone else is moving somewhere, is doing something. And the greater part of that stream of life is made up of the coolies, carrying incredible loads, walking incredible miles, working incredible hours to earn enough to live.

A STORY

In the Far East there is no harsh line drawn between the real and the apparent. A thing seems—and who knows but that it is?

For instance, I think that there was once an old man who lived in China, and that he lived in a house on a mountainside with a little courtyard cobbled with stones and a hedge of bamboo about it. Beyond his flower garden he could watch the sun set over a valley, gilding the smoke that rose from the far-off villages. A stony road wound up from this valley and passed his gate and climbed still further to a temple among the peaks. Sometimes a friend might come to sit with him before his door, drinking wine in small cups brought by a servant boy in a padded blue jacket. The servant would linger within sound of his master's laughter while the old men drank and jested or talked of life and the affairs of the kingdom.

One day one of these life-long friends brought to the old man a present, a scroll to be hung on the wall of his room. It was a painting of a horse, a little creature no higher than a hand, but stamping its little forefoot and looking out of the picture with such a living eye and such a widening of the nostril that one might have thought the tiny thing had just whinnied. The old man was delighted with it and sat before it a long time, lost in admiration of the artist's skill.

But from that moment strange things began to happen. Night

after night the old man was wakened by the sound of hoofs in his courtyard or of galloping on the road outside. He would run to the door and perhaps catch a glimpse of a far-off horse cantering along the rocky lane, or hear a wild neigh sometimes from the direction of the temple and sometimes from the lower road that led down to the valley. Yet his stable was empty, and for years no horse had stood in its stalls. At first he thought that someone must be taking an urgent message to the priests, but what could the message be that must be taken night after night after the sun had set?

Then one night as he stood with a light in his old hand, just wakened by the loud passing of the mysterious animal, his eye happened to light upon the scroll that hung on his wall.

It was blank!

Or almost so. True, a few grasses and flowers were painted there, and a tree, but no horse stood beneath it, stamping its jet-black hoof. The old man immediately understood: so truly painted had the little steed been that it had passed beyond the bounds of painting and entered into a life of its own.

Next day the old man rose early, put the scroll under his arm (after making sure that the little horse was again in its place), and walked down to the village. There he found the artist who had painted the scroll and explained the difficulty. The artist smiled and prepared his paints. In the twinkling of an eye he had painted a bridle of heavy red silk about the horse's head, and had fastened it to a bough with a strong painted red rope with a silk tassel at the end.

And from that day onward the old man was never again troubled by hoofs in the night.

THE LITTLE TOWN

It was Christmas Eve and we were alone in Macao, that charming old Portuguese town on the Pearl River, once the main port of trade with southern China till Hong Kong was built at the mouth and Macao was left to wither on her narrow harbor. It was night and the plastered walls no longer showed the blues and yellows and salmon pinks that would be seen by day; the blinds were no longer pale green. The water had lost its golden brown in blackness lighted by a few sparks of fire from the huddled river craft below the sea wall.

As our feet appeared on the stairs facing the open door of the hotel, a dozen boys dashed forward with their jinrikshas. As usual we chose the three victors despite the protests and entreaties of the others. Then we were off under the banyans to the rhythmic pad of sandaled feet. Against the sea wall the water was breaking with little licking flames of phosphorus. We pointed our boys into the city proper, down to the district of the native stores; we were out to buy Christmas presents, jokes for each others' stockings. The streets were narrow and thronging with coolies in blue and merchants in their long coats lined with turquoise-colored silk. Everywhere were entrances to gambling halls, for the greater part of the revenue that the town sends back to Portugal comes from its gambling places and opium dens, forbidden in the rest of China. We stopped at junk shops and haggled over broken bits of jade, carved soapstone, a piece or two of embroidery. There is little to buy, but there may be much fun had in buying it. Then we entered into an endurance test with our boys. We tried to express firecrackers. They tried to understand. After twenty minutes of pantomime and several false starts we arrived at a store ablaze with red, green, and gold wrappings stacked on shelves lining the entire shop. There were firecrackers of all sizes, punk, candles as red as blood twisted into strange spirals. We bought half a dozen large packages, for we knew a hill shouldering down to the sea from an ancient fort. In the morning we should sit and watch the yellow-brown sails of the junks beating out to the fishing grounds while we lighted our crackers and tossed them down towards the water far below us. Then we should go to the stairway leading up to the great façade of the ruined cathedral thin against the sky, remembering that it was the inspiration for "Cross of Christ in thee I glory, towering o'er the wrecks of time." And we should go to the park with its carefully trained banyan trees and its borders of flowers set in faience bowls.

With our 'rikshas filled with bundles we started home. Soon we were out of the crowded section and passing through narrow silent streets between high plaster walls. Above, the stars were shining down quietly: almost instinctively, we began to sing. There was not a soul in sight, only the narrow Oriental star-lit streets of a little town.

O little town of Bethlehem

—we sang, and the coolies' feet made almost no sound as they ran on—

How still we see thee lie,
Above thy deep and dreamless sleep
The silent stars go by.
Yet in thy dark streets shineth
The everlasting light,
The hopes and fears of all the years
Are met in thee tonight.

—and magic and promise of unutterable things lay all about us.

⊷§ Governments may change, and opinions, and the very appearance of lands themselves, but the slowest thing to change is religion. What has once been associated with worship becomes holy in itself, and self-perpetuating, always built upon the foundation of mingled awe and attraction which the unknown has for the mind of man. During our long journey through the Orient we saw many among the thousands of ways in which the East worships her gods and keeps alive the pageantry of the past, but the greatest contrast was between the rites at Java's mountain sacred to Brahma and the demeanor of the wandering priests of what was then Siam.

THE TEST

Captain Happé, the official Dutch adviser to the local sultan, looking like an exact replica of a brownie, told us he had seen it himself. It was many years ago in the days when the sultans of central Java had far more power than they possess today. The prince royal was gambling with a courtier. One can imagine them in one of the pavilions, squatted on the black marble in their brown and blue sarong skirts, the prince in a colored jacket with silver buttons, the other, according to kraton etiquette, naked above the waist. Attendants would doubtless have been grouped around them, probably with a dwarf to hold the box of betel nuts and the silver spittoon. Over their shoulders would have peered the gilt figures of allegorical women holding French lamps. In the court about them the sun would be blazing full on the playing children, and in some cool room beyond the arcades the sultan was probably asleep in his canopied bed, dozing away the hot hours fanned by his wives. All was very peaceful in an Oriental-tropical way. But suddenly that peace was torn through like silk ripped by daggers. The prince had cheated. And the courtier had struck him.

A few days later the court, the neighboring royalty, and the few foreign officials in the town (including Captain Happé, of course) were invited to a spectacle. Naturally there would have been many ways of getting rid of the courtier—a kris through his back for one thing, or tiger hairs passed through the grains of his rice, clipped so they did not show, if a more secret, slower death was thought desirable. It may be that the sultan wanted to give the man a sporting chance for his life.

When the visitors arrived they found a circle of the guard drawn up with spears turned in about a round open space in which stood two wooden cages. In that country it took no great cleverness to guess what they contained, and I imagine everyone was in haste to take a place well behind the soldiers. The sultan spoke to the unfortunate courtier: "You were so bold," said he, "as to strike my eldest son. See if you are so bold, my friend, as to open these two cages." It was hardly a question. The courtier saluted, that humble little gesture of the two joined hands raised to the forehead. He walked slowly through the soldiers. No one breathed. He opened the door of the first cage, squatted and saluted. Never looking behind him, he raised the door of the second cage, and again performed his slow reverence with his back to the now freed tigers. Then he walked through the circle of soldiers He had made no sudden uncontrolled motion of any kind.

The entertainment was over for the day. I imagine the guests were all offered refreshments and things were very gay in the kraton. Perhaps the younger princesses danced one of their long historical dances in which they scarcely move their feet. Everyone went home exhilarated at having grazed tragedy. But whether the courtier went on living, or disappeared in some other way, Captain Happé could not tell.

BROMO

We were far up on the slopes of the Java mountains when the sun rose in front of us, with long clouds gloriously trailing across the sky. Suddenly we were on the edge of a precipice. The land opened away before us. A thousand feet below lay the Sand Sea, almost black, and from our height perfectly smooth. Its extent was unguessable, so lost was all sense of proportion or distance. A steep wall varying from a thousand to two thousand feet lipped it squarely around. Towards the middle of the Sand Sea rose a sharp cone, and behind it another one with its top blown off, the gray and putty-red form of the Bromo. Miles and miles away behind them the beautiful cap of Smeroe lifted itself finely against the sky. No such desolation can be imagined, no such grandeur. Down a thousand feet of steep twisting trail we slid, leading our ponies; across two miles of sand we galloped while the horse-boy scurried after; and then we came to the octopus tentacles of the sacred crater Bromo, or Brahma, writhing gray and red from the central cone, and walked up the flight of stairs almost buried in sand to the crater's black gullet. The lava barked far below in its caverns. There was a cloud of smoke rising from it. The swallows flew about the ledge, and the Javanese boy, having tied the ponies, performed horrible deeds of daring along the crumbling edge while we shouted unheeded orders for him to return.

Not so many years ago it had been the custom of the native princes to send human sacrifices to this appalling spot. One can imagine the procession, in the somewhat tarnished grandeur that seems to cling to tropical princelings, winding across the Sand Sea and up that steep slope of the volcano, with the bedecked sacrifice moving unwillingly in the center.

We looked out over the bed of that ancient and vaster crater and saw that a group of men was indeed coming towards us in single file. They walked steadily and had soon climbed to the ledge beside us, in silence, paying no heed to our presence. There were seven of them, elderly men, in sarongs and white jackets, who must have come from one of the three hamlets which still worship Brahma in a Mohammedan country. They walked to a point overhanging the crater; the oldest squatted, with the others grouped behind him. Silently he lighted a bundle of straw filled with incense. Silently he threw into the depth of the crater little packages of rice and flowers and small coins wrapped in green leaves. Then he threw in the still-burning bundle of straw and incense, rose with expressionless face, and, followed by the six other old men, walked swiftly down the mountain into the great basin of sand hemmed in by the high mountain rim. Their figures grew small in the distance, and we were left alone in the desolate presence of the god.

THE CROWS OF CHANG WAT

Across the crowded river from Bangkok stands the temple Chang Wat like a porcelain diadem for some Titan mandarin. Its halls and towers are all flowers of plaster or china, as bright as an old-fashioned bouquet, as fresh as a teacup, as great as a cathedral. At sunset under a sky of pulsing gold the rooks caw about the galleries, accursed and mocking, yet with a black wistfulness beneath their savage irony. They may be the same birds whom Brother Simon of Assisi, at prayer in the woods, bade begone forever that they might no longer disturb his devotions. Only Odin, the fierce god of blue cold skies, snowstorms, and wolves, ever sheltered them, raising them to stand before his throne. Valhalla is long since overthrown, and now the crows are whirled like black leaves over the world, masterless, a dark pattern across the serene flush of the tropic sky.

THE YELLOW PRIESTS

The priests of Siam go dressed in yellow with begging bowls in their hands, for yellow was the dress of humility, of outcasts and beggars, and their Master wore it in India more than two thousand years ago. The priests stop at the doors of the little shops of Bangkok. Many of them are boys and wear the robe only for a few years, and if the hands that pour out the rice into the polished bowl be young and pretty, so much the better. The priests pass along the streets among the Chinese craftsmen and the Siamese, men and women chewing and spitting the red juice of betel nuts. There are shops of the fashioners of gods, and shops filled with krisses with silver handles, and shops of baskets and shops where tiger skins hang in the dust. But all killing is cruel, think the yellow priests as they go serenely by with their begging bowls in their hands. The Buddha himself was once a tiger. It was when he had won his princess in open competition with the other princes, having ridden the horse they could not ride; having shot more skillfully than they could shoot, and swung the sword they could not swing that he said to his bride under her gold-and-black-barred veil, "Thou rememberest, O most beautiful, by thy veil, I see that thou rememberest how I, a tiger, won thee, a tigress, in the jungle many births ago." It is wrong to kill, think the yellow priests, bending their heads as they pass.

The streets are wide and the runners pass by, and the elephant of the king goes down to bathe in the river; the sun shines hot, the children run naked through the crowd that puts them aside gently; the courtiers pass in their sarongs colored according to the day. Unjostled in the midst move the priests with their begging bowls in their hands, folded in humility. And yet their Master was not always humble: there are temples to him where he lies as a prince covered with jewels, and with his feet inlaid with mystic symbols laid in mother-of-pearl. The temples are more gorgeous than any palace; they are like rainbows that have been turned into spires, tapering and delicate; they are more fantastic than cloud shapes; they have roof piled upon roof and are upheld by pillars bizarre and gleaming like jewels. Only the yellow figures of the priests may be seen moving to and fro on the paths, the humble priests returned from their begging. And around them lies the jungle, fold on fold, green wall upon green wall, where the birds cry and apes hang in the branches and the snakes coil in the roots, and the elephants go feeding majestically, raising their heads now and then to trumpet. Yet such was the love of Buddha for all things, that all things brought him love in return. When he sat in the jungle so deep in the mystery of thought that he could not rouse himself for food, it was the thoughtless apes and the elephants who brought him wild honey in the comb and fruit from jungle trees. Even the animals, the righteous say, have pity upon the priests as they walk like staid yellow dreams with their begging bowls in their hands.

The day deepens and darkens; yellow like the yellow of the priests' robes spreads in the sky and lies reflected in the broad river. The country people return to jungle villages with their unsold produce; noblemen under awnings languidly watch the light catch along the crests of the ripples, and fishermen return with their nets heaped in the prow and the bottom of their boats filled with slippery gold as the sunset falls across the bodies of the catch. But in the water before the temples the fish unconcernedly leap for blundering moths. No fishing boat puts off from those shallows, for had not the Buddha also been a fish and entered into the sufferings and thoughts of a fish? Under the shelter of his pitying robe they may live at peace. "Peace, peace," say the priests, kneeling like yellow shadows before the altars: "Peace, peace."

Journeys from Chimney Farm

1930–1968

In 1929 came a break in my life. Travel had been my greatest joy. It continued to have a place, but the focus of my life changed. Marriage was a deeper fulfillment, the birth of a child more exciting than any journey.

Henry and I became engaged one January day before I started for California. The next six months were very happy and busy times for us both. He went to England and saw The Outermost House through the press. I wrote The Cat Who Went to Heaven, which was later to be awarded a Newbery Medal, and with Margaret went to Copán, that wonderful and at that time rarely visited ruin in what was then British Honduras. We hired mules and were gone for three or four days, sleeping in the hammocks which we carried tied to our saddles. I remember as very strange that in those high mountains we were warned to look out for alligators if we bathed in the stream which the trail crossed and recrossed. Margaret bathed anyway, while I stood nervously watching for alligators.

Then came the return, first to California and then to Hingham, where Henry and I were married in Morton and Margaret's house. We spent two weeks at the Fo'castle, where he had written The Outermost House, and then sailed for a summer in England.

Our first daughter was born at the end of June 1930, and the second nearly two years later, so that the nurse carried her to Chimney Farm, near the Maine coast, in a market basket padded and lined with rose-sprigged dimity. We had meanwhile bought the farm overlooking Damariscotta Pond. "And when I buy a house there will be nothing between it and the view," said Henry, nor has there ever been, unlike dear Shipcote with a road unseen but not unheard below its hedges as one looked out to Hingham Harbor and far-off Boston Light.

I was thirty-six years old when I married and Henry was five years older, so that for both of us it was very much of an adventure and we embarked upon it gaily and warmly. At the same time, writing remained of great importance to us both.

SOUTH SHORE

I say that almost everywhere there is beauty enough to fill a person's life if one would only be sensitive to it. But Henry says No: that broken beauty is only a torment, that one must have a whole beauty with man living in relation to it to have a rich civilization and art, and he cites the exhibit we have just left, the shallow paintings without imagination, without anything to say, where only the still-lifes had real power in their narrow field. And he goes on, "Thin soil—this country is all glacier-thin soil, and that smeared over with an industrial civilization." And Fore-and-Aft, our little Ford, speeds on, picking her way accurately and neatly in and out of traffic, past run-down residence districts and the wastes of the city dump over the blue bay; and the spring wind is flapping the papers and the seagulls are circling above with the light on their breasts and wings, and the smoke of the smoldering dump-fires hangs low and flat as though from funeral pyres; and I remember the blowing manes of dump horses on a background of gas tanks and blue water. And something in me cries, 'This is beautiful too, this is strange and beautiful. And the little Ford, always neatly and accurately, glides on in and out among other cars, overtaken and overtaking, like one herring in a school of springtime herring, and we pass the Neponset Bridge and the view up to the Blue Hills which alone Henry loves; but I look, too, on to the city across the swamps where it stands in a sunset light of towers and smoke across water that is faded lavender, and at the great waters of Quincy Shore where the duck come, and the first flashes of Boston Light begin above the mirage-like pattern of the islands.

Is it because I am a woman that I accept what crumbs I may have, accept the hot-dog stands and amusement parks if I must, if the blue is bright beyond them and the sunset flushes the breasts of the sea birds? But Henry will not compromise: more foolish or more wise, he demands a harmony of elements, and to this unwillingness to accept the slurred and scratchy outlines of the usual suburban landscape, I owe the weeks at the Fo'castle and the Farm.

HENRY WILLIAMSON

Henry Williamson spent the night at Shipcote, a harried, sad-eyed man, tall, bent, with badger hair and a face like the photographs of Masefield. His wife was much younger, perhaps a Cornish type, with wide dark brows, very simple and quiet in her manner. They had with them a young American couple who were interviewing them, and they seemed tired and at bay. We served a high tea that had been ready for some hours; I noticed that he particularly liked the little pâté-de-foi-gras sandwiches. Afterwards in the south room with a fire on the hearth he asked if he might read, and soon became absorbed in an old *Vanity Fair*. But finding himself left alone, he bit by bit joined the conversation. The reporter and her husband went home. We talked of England. He was pleased when I said that English landscape often seemed to have horizons that rolled down, most places having horizons that roll up and enclose them. Later he was speaking of New York and how discouraged he had been there and of the suicide of his closest friend in London. "At the time I was very close to it myself," he said. I noticed Mrs. Williamson's fingers grip, hand tightly laced in hand. They have two little boys and a ten-months-old Margaret at home in England. I pitied her life with a husband always living with the dead. There is a little tic of mouth and eyes that tells its story.

In a deep dreaming voice he recited Wilfred Owen's poetry,

which Henry took up, once more surprising me. There were primroses in a glass vase on their bureau, their sheets smelled of lavender and tea appeared on their breakfast tray. I scarcely saw them in the morning except to shake hands, when he said rather pathetically, "I've felt more at home here than in any place in America. May I come back for a few days if I lecture in Boston?" But he was not to come back.

RETURN TO
THE OUTERMOST HOUSE

We are always coming and going to the Cape from our winter headquarters at Shipcote. The most beautiful thing in these six last weeks was a day spent at the Fo'castle. I joined Henry on a Saturday noon, and after lunch at the Kelleys' we walked again the outer beach. The waves came from a bank of fog and as always the restriction of the horizon added to instead of decreased the sense of immensity. Far ahead of us we saw the roof of the Fo'castle cocked against the sky. Only that and the long swell of the dunes, for the other two cottages that had been built on the nearer heights had been carried away in the high tides of March, and their wreckage mingled with the strewn seaweed, lobster pots, painted buoys, and planks that were heaped in the cuts.

We gathered many armfuls of firewood to make us safe against a cold night: a chair leg, or a buoy marked *Wincapaw* from Maine; birch saplings from one of the weirs, pieces of plank. I wanted to take back a thick piece of bamboo, ten feet long, shining and oriental. Once a bubble of light caught our glance and we found a glass floater, and that we rescued for the mantel. So bit by bit, side by side, we heaped up our woodpile, and, leaving a good fire to warm the room, walked on to the cut beyond and the great bared bones of the wreck which used to be half covered with sand a little north of us and now has been carried a quarter of a mile or more to the south to lie starkly in the open under the newly shaped dunes of the cut. Everything looked sharper and wilder from the chiseling of the storm. Even now we faced into a strong wind and felt the white spray in our faces.

The Fo'castle seemed charming. Hulled corn was cooked on the coals, and the kettle boiled against the lick of the flames. There were the windows opening on the marshes where large flocks of eider duck were drifting with the tide, observing one another in the preliminary stages of courtship.

As it grew darker inside, our candles and lamp turned the room to yellow. The big bed was spread wide before the fire and we gathered pillows and books. Such an air of remoteness and well-being filled us! All night we slept warm beside our fire with the ocean calling at our door through the darkness and fog.

Next morning through a light rain we returned rather unwillingly to Shipcote and Hingham.

RECESSION AT SHIPCOTE

It is after six o'clock and the babies are both in bed after a family tea party on the lawn, but still the late sun shines across Mrs. Long's meadow like a pink wafer in a watermelon fog. I shall be forty this spring but I am still young enough to be moved by the changes of light, and the feeling of air on my bare arms in this sudden summer that is bringing the fruit trees into hurried bud. Henry has gone to the Cape to see that the Fo'castle is in order for the recluse who has rented it for May.

Meanwhile our anxiety centers on Shipcote. These days are curious ones: the appearances remain the same, but the props are giving way one by one beneath the foundations of our civilization. Henry spoke of migrations at the Terrys' the other evening. I looked about the supper table afterwards at all the people so gaily dressed and so gaily talking together. A man from Mars would surely not have guessed the strain that lay just beneath that gaiety, but we all knew that at least three of the families represented were scarcely sure where they should turn for the commonest necessities. As far as we are concerned the strain should be much lighter. But I take things too hard, I think. All winter I have been worrying and budgeting, mulling figures over and over in my mind, trying to shrink expenses to fit our shrinking income. This is all new to me! I learn my lesson painfully and spend too much fire on it, and this winter I have been tired and anxious and duller than I should have been to the unchanging delights and satisfactions of life.

But now for the first time I feel the relief that spring brings after a winter lived through; of the need for coal (that bugaboo) diminishing; of the farm ahead with its lessening expenses; of a birthday check to be expected. A robin's egg lies broken and blue at the foot of a tree; a hawk soars past, harshly calling; the violets have poked out their folded hoods; Meg is saying all the nursery rhymes; Pussy is holding safety-pins to help anyone changing her diapers; the southwest wind has begun to blow through elms and maples tasseled with flowers. I shall not let myself wonder if we belong to a class doomed to a slow destruction, or hope that we now stand at the bottom of the ladder and that things will resume again something of their old stability.

"Away, dull care!" The southwest wind is blowing and once more the infant maples are sprouting on the lawn.

MOTHER AT CHIMNEY FARM

As I sit here at Chimney Farm, hearing the cuckoo clock and Henry's motions in the next room, the occasional snap of his fire, the movements of the gray cat in the opposite chair and the buzz of the too-numerous flies, I find myself thinking of Mother.

Who shall ever put down her personality, so unassuming and gentle, so open to new times and manners, so obstinate, so dependent on her daughters, so self-respecting, so indifferent to the world in general, so shrewd, so vague, so generous? Who will tell of her carefully polished shoes, of her love for sunsets, of her gloves necessary and mislaid, of her love for thick cream and apple pie, of her pretty blue eyes, of her lefthanded sewing, of her care in making a bed, of her abstracted reading of the newspaper, of her fondness for lilies of the valley, or her hatred for cooking, of her courage under pain, of her passion for new countries, and of the endless light whispering slap of her cards playing solitaire, that resource for the person left alone in his generation among those of a later birth?

Something in her forbids her to worry much over anything. When the lightning and thunder struck above the farm she went to bed in her best nightgown, "in case anything should happen," she explained.

How kind she is, but not at all uncritical, spending her dearest love on her immediate family, the pleasant-faced, straight-backed, young-bodied woman with the blue eyes and the pretty waving white hair on her head that is round and firm as a cat's; she who was always sure (even when they were most annoying) that her children "would turn out all right"; who never pitied herself in the years of life with a masterful mother-in-law; who, in spite of a charming manner, hated meeting strangers and shrank from social contacts (unless bulwarked by a daughter); her fear of ever being a trouble; well, in short, that is she, sitting smiling and quiet in the corner of the sofa in a black dress with blue lapels, the handkerchief in her sleeve smelling of Quelques Fleurs—that is she whom everyone always calls "Mother Coatsworth."

WRITING

After Henry and I settled here at the farm in Maine we did a great deal of writing. He wrote long and beautifully balanced books—*Northern Farm, The St. Lawrence*, and *Herbs and the Earth*—as well as two anthologies, one of Maine writers, *White Pine and Blue Water*, and another of selections from contemporary accounts of America from the earliest times to the present, called *American Memory*. And then I mustn't forget *Henry Beston's Fairy Tales*, some of them taken from two earlier books of fairy tales, often much rewritten, with later stories added to them.

Before he wrote any book he "sat for a long time considering his navel," as he used to say. When at last he felt ready, he always had a publisher's contract at hand, and a kitchen table.

There were many kitchen tables, one in the kitchen, one in the so-called library, one in the herb attic above my bedroom where he had a stove too, and a spool-bed to lie on to listen to the rain on the slanting roof close overhead, and one in the little building which was also his study and once stood close to the barn where he could oversee the house when the children were little and might suddenly need him. Later this was moved close to a grove of trees near the lake with additions and a window that filled the entire water-side wall, and this, too, had its cot and its stove—a very small one which he had bought on the south shore of the St. Lawrence and which was intended for the cabin of a small sloop or tugboat.

At all of those tables he wrote, always with pencils which he kept very sharp, always on large loose sheets of paper which were lucky if they didn't find themselves crunched up into a ball and thrown over his shoulder onto the floor. Only a few joined the stack which grew slowly at one end of the table. He was a meticulous writer, using a thesaurus and dictionary when he needed them. Occasionally an entire morning's work would be spent on a single sentence.

"Why don't you go on, and come back to it later?" I might suggest, passing by and seeing how many popcorn-balls of paper lay on the floor and how yesterday's page was still on top of the pile. But Henry always answered, "I can't go on until I am perfectly satisfied with a sentence." Such was his manner of work, and those who read his books know how well he was justified in it.

But as for me, it was a different matter. I never had a contract. Before we were married I had used a Corona portable, but Henry felt that the rattle of the keys destroyed all natural rhythms of the mind so I wrote with a pencil too, or in later days with a ballpoint pen. I never used loose leaves but always school composition books with lined paper so that I could keep track of where I was. The idea for some stories appeared complete in my brain; some lay fallow for years. In either case they were written at top speed. Often I recognized that a sentence or a paragraph might be shaky but I would go right on, planning to come back to it later when I could see the chapter as a whole. In many cases I never did go back. The shaky sentence remains shaky to the end. But I had had good training in writing poetry, where every word counts, and the wrong word cannot take the place of the right one. Even when writing at top speed I think I was selective. I began to create a style, on the very simple premise that the writing should be as clear as glass and allow the subject to show through, with as little emphasis on the writer as possible. To this end whenever I could I chose words with Anglo-Saxon rather than Latin derivations.

Over the years my subconscious became more and more a

factor, as it learned the rules. The time came—I cannot give a date for it—when my subconscious took most of the responsibility. I would find myself taking dictation from it. Writing was an intoxication.

I never wrote—or write—except between breakfast and luncheon, and if Henry was not writing I was prepared to leave my work at the first suggestion of his wishing us to do something together.

Writing was for me an addiction like drink, which I kept as much as possible out of sight.

And how fast I worked! I counted on forty hours as enough for most of my small books. My *Cat Who Went to Heaven* was written the winter before marriage while Henry was in England "seeing *The Outermost House* through the press," and I was in a summer cottage by the Pacific with my mother's family about to join my sister Margaret on a trip to Guatemala, at that time almost unspoiled by the blight of tourism. I had a little extra time on my hands, so I remembered the temple of Borobudur in Java and a picture in a Kyoto temple and with a little added here and there, worked hard for a week and finished *The Cat*, typed it and illustrated it crudely with drawings which Lynd Ward used later as a basis for his beautiful work. And that week, besides writing the book, I did my share of the housework, not including cooking, about which I knew nothing.

But already the habit of writing fast and accurately was fully developed. My real training was in poetry. In those days of rhyme, when even free verse was careful of its rhythms, that muse was a demanding one, if often dissatisfied. All these years I have relied upon it, although I know that now, along with my conscious mind, it grows slipshod. It is still a muse, even if only a small one.

LUCK

What is luck? I don't know. Fate, I suppose. Probably luck is with me many times a day, when I do not slip on the linoleum or hit the car that appears suddenly from a driveway. The only bingo game I ever played was on the little passenger-freighter sailing down the St. Lawrence on which Henry took us, stopping every day at some harbor to put off and take on freight, making her way through the Straits of Belle Isle, where I saw my first iceberg, and as far as Battle Harbour in Labrador. I had never played bingo before and have never played again, but I won enough to invite everyone at the table to the ship's bar for a drink, and later to buy from an antique dealer on Charles Street in Boston an old Delft blue pitcher shaped like a monkey with the words in Dutch on its stomach, "What's good in the mouth, agrees with the belly."

When Margaret and I gambled a little Chinese money in Portuguese Macao we both won; I think it was a come-hither gesture on the part of the management, although as such it failed. I have never gambled since.

These small isolated fliers in gambling never gave me any sense at all that the Fates were interested in me, but twice things have occurred that seemed really lucky.

Once during the year that Mother, Margaret, and I spent in the Far East, we went to see where a Javanese palace had stood. The only thing I remember as still standing—if you could call it standing—was a large well in which lived two great tortoises believed to be the spirits of the last emperor and empress. One bought little pieces of meat wrapped in a bit of banana leaf and threw it into the well. If a tortoise rose for it, it brought the thrower great luck.

We bought our little chunks of meat, and Mother and Margaret both threw and nothing happened. Then I threw mine and out of the depths a tortoise rose. It was like the ones seen in Chinese and Japanese embroideries, with a long green tail of seaweed waving from its ancient shell. As I remember, its beaked head was white with age. It rose, was for a moment visible, took the offering, and retired into the depths of the royal well. The vendor congratulated me. I saw several Javanese throw in their bits of meat, but no tortoise rose to take them. As we walked away, I felt that fate had smiled on me, a small smile, perhaps an unmeaning smile, but still a smile.

I had the same feeling many years later when Henry and I spent a few days in Mérida, the capital of Yucatán. I don't remember how we came to be with Americans in a house owned by some of them: we probably had presented a letter of introduction. Somehow our hosts brought out a hunk of copal and put it on a round coffee table and lighted it. It is still sacred among the Maya and is secretly burned as an offering to the old gods. Whomever the smoke sought out would be blessed.

I think that there were seven or eight of us around the table, and the smoke chose me. Incidentally, it had a very pleasant odor. I felt that there must be a draft in the room that caused the smoke to come in my direction, so I moved at least forty-five degrees into a new position. The smoke followed me, and once again wrapped itself about me in a light cocoon.

Everyone laughed and said, "You're lucky," and we moved away and the host covered the copal—which is precious even today—so that the fire would go out. Once more I felt that I had been honored. By whom or by what? That I don't know.

But twice in my life the genius of a place has rewarded my delight in it, twice the oracle has spoken. And that will do me.

LIGHT AND SHADE

I love brilliant sunlight seen through deep shadow. Before the first World War a German firm published posters. One was of a young man sitting on the ground with his back against the trunk of a pine tree. Deep shadow fell on him and all about him but he looked out onto a landscape bathed in light. I sometimes think of that painting as I drive past a small pine wood near our farmhouse. A young woman, now dead, cleared out all the underbrush and that bristle of dead branches close to the ground, and glancing at it the eye is drawn past whole layers of deepest shadow to sunlight beyond the trunks.

Or one may be delighted by the light and shade in another combination. Now and then a heavy shower passes over our road eastward beyond the lake and its dark shores. The clouds will mass in a black wall there on the other side, while the sunshine strikes the fields on this side, and every grass-blade, weed, and flower in them, to a wet and burning green. A tremulous rainbow hangs against the clouds. Looking out through your skull's two windows you know you are seeing a beauty rare and certain to be gone in a moment. It is one of the miracles of daily life that you should see it at all. It is, surely, an enchantment more fit for the eyes of magicians than for everyday human beings like ourselves.

MASTERS OF ART

There are four sounds in the room: the hiss and snap of flame, the droning tick of the old Friesland clock, the occasional turning of the leaf of a book, and the steady small surge of a moving pen.

Henry's voice comes suddenly from his chair by the fire where he is looking at art books.

"There's one thing I'd like to see," he remarks, "and that's a fight between one of Rosa Bonheur's dogs and Landseer's."

"Which would win?" I ask idly from the desk.

"Rosa's," he says with certainty. "They're nastier." Henry with his passionate love of wild animals is no lover of dogs.

Comparative silence returns. The leaves of the old bound copies of *Masters of Art* whisper again under a straying hand. The next time he speaks it is in a different voice.

"I have always wanted to walk through the arches of this Van Eyck," he says, "and into the city beyond. Do you remember the one I mean? No man has ever imagined a lovelier place."

How well I do remember it with its river and distant bridge, its walks and fair houses minutely blossoming under Van Eyck's brush, less suave but more beautiful than those Italian landscapes seen from the open windows of Annunciations, through the broken arches of Nativities, or beyond the crosses of Calvary. What eternal tranquillity rests upon the tiny figures that move in those secret worlds forever undisturbed by any breath of wind or troubling of emotion.

But already Henry has passed to other things and is busy with the Dutch.

"They knew how to enjoy life," he remarks. "The things they cared for were simplicity, music, domestic gaiety, good painting, and clean floors all enjoyed at a proper tempo. Living was an art and not a slavery with them. They had a sense of the human values. That is the true test. Yet no one of my favorite painters is Dutch. Who do I like best? Velasquez, Dürer, Holbein and Fra Angelico."

I say, taking up the game, "Mine would be Vermeer and Goya and the drawings of Ingres." But I stop, growing confused by rival claims. Do I like the brothers Le Nain so much because I know them less well? And Breughel the Younger? But am I not choosing little Masters, or at least littler Masters? If I had a palace I would want a Tintoretto. I ponder and return to my letter while the fire continues to crumble and the old clock in the corner methodically winds its shuttle of time.

There is a much longer silence. Many, many pages are turned behind me in the lamp-lit room, while my mind wanders from the paper narcissus shaking out its flowers above me, to bills, and the friend whose letter lies open on the blotter. Is there a smell of sage still on those pages, and do ranges of barren mountains rim their margins? How I love that land and hate its present phase, what memories rise in me of former delights and distastes!

I have gone far from the long, low room walled on one side with windows and on the other with books.

But Henry moves and replaces a heavy volume.

"I could never be an expatriate," he says. "There are too many religious paintings in Europe." As he develops his theme his voice deepens:

> *Too many martyrdoms,*
> *   Golgothas everywhere.*
> *After the first few cities and*
> *   the first hundred churches*

that kind of art lays me low.
I weary of attitudinizing
            saints
rolling the whites of their
            eyes at God the Father,
of those skies pink
            with the backsides
            of baby angels
in whose midst a tiaraed
            presence
has materialized looking
            uncommonly
            like a Protestant;
of too many softly
            athletic young
            gentlemen
clad only in diapers and
            bound to a tree
all eyes, arrows and sighs.
If I see another Nativity,
            I shall kick a lamb.
I am sick of bearded
            venerables in the corners
            of great canvases
each in a fit.
No, I quite genuinely
            prefer "Washington
Crossing the Delaware."

I put the stopper in the ink bottle and turn from the desk. And there is Henry in his favorite chair, his head outlined on a background of books, his eyes bright with mischief.

AT A TANGENT

I think sometimes that when Henry and I die, Henry will go knowing that he has given an exact impression of the world and life as he has seen it, but that I shall know that I have left behind me only glimpses, random remarks, things seen at a tangent. Is it the difference of our temperaments that explains this? Or do all women live from spark to spark, as they might walk through a meadow of fireflies, content to say, "At this moment I was happy. As we passed the window my little girl exclaimed, and looking out I saw a hundred seagulls wheel across the sky above the icy bay, the sunset rosy on their breasts"?

FELICITY

One of the things we constantly hear from all the farmers is about sleeping so they can hear the stock. Any discussion of a house is sure to include, "I sleep in such-and-such a chamber, so I can be near the stock and hear if anything goes wrong in the night."

When a lightning storm begins after dark the farmers and their wives always dress, to be ready to save the stock if the barn is struck. Fire; the unknown—one begins to fear the things that the farmer fears. And one understands more and more their helplessness before bad neighbors or tramps. Each man is so isolated. He does not dare make enemies: someone may dig up his potatoes, but the farmer does not dare voice his suspicions; someone may carry away one of his sheep, but he does not dare rouse bad blood, that may end in a burning barn or a fire in his woods.

Henry has come in, and has put a frying pan on the stove. Something will soon be cooking for lunch and I shall be laying the dishes on the checked tablecloth we bought at Head Tide this summer and which I hemmed. He is in his English golf trousers and a dark blue woolen shirt. I am wearing a mulberry-colored dress and one of the bright rainbow-striped aprons popular this year. But it is hard to find any expression for the air of quiet intimacy and warmth that fills the house, flowing silently from one of us to the other, and back again, a domestic current like the circulation of blood.

As I sat here earlier, sewing back the edging of the fine African mat that Mother and Margaret and I bought years ago at the Wembley Exhibit outside London, and which now lies in my farm study and is hurt by the rub of my desk chair moving back and forth—as I sat quietly sewing while Henry was drawing water at the well, I planned idly the beginning of a fairy story.

"What is the matter with you, O needle!" the woman exclaimed at last, "that you so often elude my thread?"

And the needle answered her, "Because, dear Mistress, the garment upon which you are sewing is a garment of ill-omen."

And when she began sweeping the hearth the broom handle kept twisting out of her hand and the broom kept clattering to the floor.

"What is the matter with you, O broom?" the woman exclaimed at last, "that you keep twisting from my hand and clattering to the floor?"

And the broom answered her, "Because, dear Mistress, the guest for whom you sweep the stone of the hearth, is a guest of ill-omen."

So the mind amuses itself while the hands are quietly busy. And now a few flakes of snow are falling and Henry is putting on the storm windows, not three feet away. I must get Bee's recipe and make some fudge. It is the only way I know to find an expression for the mood of felicity in which I sit here.

LES FLEURS DE LA VIE

The magic of the autumn has seized the countryside; now that the sun isn't ripening anything it shines for the sake of the golden age; for the sake of Eden; to please the moon for all I know. Even Meg feels it, and yesterday dragged me to see a cow because of the blanket of light on her back. "See the fire colors in the trees," says Meg.

Henry is finishing his herb book in a rush like a horse going up a hill. I am galloping along beside, being secretary. I feel stirred by the warmth of so much beauty created so near at hand; I watch the lake through the window, the bright blue ruffled lake.

He's working now by the lamp in the next room and I sit here with Mother and Bos'n, the black bull terrier, and the sleeping gray cat, writing. But daytimes I work in my room and Pussy pokes in her curly head and says gravely in her talking-doll voice, "Mummy's busy," and goes away, and I hear her voice in the distance, "I sink that's mine," the younger child's immemorial cry.

Sometimes of course we do things. Today we piled into the old roadster and drove to town, Mother and Henry and I (I had a new red hat on to furbish up my spring tweeds), and Henry spoke on migrations of birds and fish and insects to thirty or forty wives of legionnaires on the third floor of the Damariscotta Five-and-Ten Cent Store, in the Sportsman's Club room with its big stove and deer heads and stuffed owls and a few enormous pieces of leather furniture designed for giants. Henry spoke so well and looked so handsome; the ladies vibrated with suppressed nods. I saw their heads in front of me moving, now one, then another, as he touched on their own experiences. Afterwards they gave us coffee and heaped-up plates of chocolate and orange cake like that served at a church supper, bending over us, friendly and moved.

Then out into the cold bright air to buy groceries; and on to look at a secondhand Franklin stove and a man's fur coat, but the woman who had advertised them in the local paper was not at home. We drove back through a legendary glow of light to find that the babies and the girls had been making popcorn balls in the kitchen.

"Les fleurs de la vie."

CAR GAME

I thought everyone played the game of creating a landscape with
surnames, but I find that many people have never heard of such
an amusement to shorten a dull drive. The trouble with it perhaps is that it is all background with very little action, but the
number of possible scenes and characters is infinite.

For instance, out of a silence as we are driving, Henry may
say, "A knight——"

And if I'm quick I may add smartly, "And his leman."

"Are you sure?" Henry questions me at once.

"Yes, I've come across it several times in the newspaper spelled
with two *n*'s."

"Let it pass," Henry says magnanimously. "Are riding down
a lane——"

"Out of the hills," say I.

"Into a beautiful *green*——"

"Vale."

"Through fields——"

"Of uncut hay."

"Towards the many *rivers*—I've never seen it in the singular."

"The plural is all right. Where stands a mill——"

"With the miller——"

"By the door."

"Question!"

"So do I, but I think it sounds familiar."

"Well, I admit I shouldn't be surprised to be introduced to Mr. Joseph Door."

"To go on: Scratching the back of a big hog——"

"I know a Governor Hogg and the many jokes there used to be about his daughters Ima and Ura. By the way, one of those daughters recently gave a collection of paintings to some museum. I was pleased to see her name in print again."

"Ima or Ura?"

"I don't remember. Let's see: Scratching a hog as he watched a bird fly up——"

"Towards the wood."

That gives you the idea. It can go on for a long time, although there aren't many usable verbs. One "burns down a house," and of course there's the "backhouse" too (how that name persists in all its spellings!). You can Dare this or that (remember poor Virginia) but I don't think there are many verbs. You have a great choice of characters besides Miller and Knight and Leman: there are Shepherds and Riders and the Rich and Poor and Shoemakers and Tanners, and Younghusbands—oh, the list is endless as you will find if you try the game, and the landscapes can vary a good deal. But after a few minutes we usually drift off into general conversation or get to our destination and the game comes to a natural end. We never play it in the house, or with pencils and paper. To be fun it must be al fresco.

OH, YOU WILL, WILL YOU?

Henry liked to attend services in the beautiful Episcopal church by the river in Newcastle, especially because he liked the rector, Father Venno, so much, and thought the service so beautiful. I went too, and thought parts of the service beautiful, but when he could no longer kneel and rise with the congregation we stopped going. All during my Episcopalian years I continued to sit on the pew during prayers and only bowed my head to a hand laid on the back of the seat in front of me. That was my Presbyterian bringing-up. In any case, I was never a natural churchgoer. Even Henry was not really religious; his church attendance was for aesthetic reasons. I have noticed that people who are not religious are usually very superstitious.

Henry was.

Let's see. He thought it brought bad luck to put shoes on a bed. I suspect that this was an idea invented by a mother. Of course he never counted the carriages or cars that followed a hearse. He was a little wary on Friday the thirteenth. For years he had an idea that fifty-three was a crucial number in his life. He said, calmly, that he would die at fifty-three; when he showed no signs of dying then, he felt he had made a mistake: he would die in 1953. Again it was merely a fact, not a fear. As again it didn't happen, he dropped the idea, or apparently did.

And he never said, "I'm going to New York." Instead he would say, "I should like to go to New York"; or better still, "If all goes well, I plan to go to New York." He tried to avoid giving Fate the chance to say, "Oh, you will, will you?" and I have picked up the habit of qualified statements.

WITHOUT REASON

Kate, our younger daughter, was to be married in August and at Henry's suggestion she and I left home in May for Scandinavia for a small European fling before she settled down to be a housewife. This day we were on our way to a little Danish castle to which an elderly king had once retired with the elderly dancer who was his mistress, and there he fished in the moat, sitting in an armchair on the covered drawbridge with the lady beside him. They must have done many other things during their long retirement besides fish in the moat, but memory is selective. I see him, with wig a little on one side, and her, with her embroidery in hand. They kept no state.

So Kate and I drove slowly through a flat landscape under a blue sky. Far in the distance we could see the rim of the sea. Suddenly we came upon a barrow in a field. There are many barrows in Denmark; the Danes seem to respect these tombs of their ancestors. This had no especial features and I should think it was the monument of an ordinary man, a farmer or run-of-the-mill Viking. A greyhound or two might mingle its bones with his, and perhaps his riding horse, but there would not be the skeletons of servants or concubines in such an unpretentious grave.

For some reason we stopped the car and walked across the open field to the barrow. It was nothing but a green rectangle with perpendicular sides ten or twelve feet high. During the centuries a slight crumbling in one place made it possible for us to haul ourselves up, I with the help of Kate, and once on top we surveyed our kingdom, which was only a green rectangle of grass suspended above a green field. Why was there such a magic about it? We ate a sober little lunch of bread and cheese and drank a thermos of coffee, looking about us. Then we lay flat, gazing up at the sky. Two skylarks were singing against the blue, straight overhead, above our magic carpet. I remember it all, because I was so happy—happy without an especial reason, perhaps the best kind of happiness.

REST

Now the farm has quieted like a pool when the duck have flown away: Margaret and Morton and Mother left for Hingham yesterday early in the Buick heaped up like a gypsy caravan; Henry and I spent the whole day at the card table in my room going over his herb book, and in the afternoon we drove through the bright glowing woods, bright even under the gray sky, to mail it in Waldoboro. On the dark return a cold opening in the clouds rayed out in a green-gray light which Henry called the Eye of God gone blind, and I remember nearly running us into the water at the sawmill causeway while watching it. In the late evening I raised my shade and looked out to a pale and baleful swale of light along the southern horizon, only making one the more aware of the flat lowering of clouds above it, though a big star flickered in our northern cat's-head apple tree.

Today I have rested. Olga is once more in control; the household is diminished—I am not pushed on by its many needs. I lay in a long chair on the open verandah in Henry's big fur coat, the lap robe over my knees, and Bos'n lying stretched along the wall. The cat came like a gray shadow, with the green of the grass showing through the winking slits of his eyes; Henry came; Meg all in red like little Jacqueline Frost came, and drew pictures of a cat and dog.

ONCE UPON A TIME

Henry and I have always played games together. Today has been scorching hot, and I bought half a pound of cherries as we shopped down the brick block of Damariscotta. Henry ate one.

"Once upon a time a man threw a cherrystone into the middle of a road and it grew and grew until it obstructed traffic and a policeman——"

"Had to come and shoot it," I ended.

"That's the right ending exactly!" cried Henry, delighted.

"And I have another. Once upon a time there was a man walking on a lake and he stumbled over a drifting log and fell in and if there hadn't been a boat there, he might have drowned."

We got into the car and drove through waves of heat into the next town, Waldoboro, the car's radiator boiling over on the long hill. I tried my hand.

"Once upon a time there was a woman making an omelet and she threw the eggshells into the sink and they didn't so she sent for the plumber and had the old thing taken out. Is that all right, or does it depend too much on the pun?"

"It's all right. It's crazy," said Henry. We walked to the antique shop to pay for the hanging bookcase he bought me last week, the old Waldoboro German bookcase carved with hearts and stars and moss-rosebuds which is now the pride of our guest room.

"Once upon a time there was a little bird who loved another bird but she chose someone else to be the papa of her eggs and that made him cynical and he became a weathervane."

I don't think Henry heard the bird one at all. His attention was focused on the antique dealer. He wanted to buy an old book for a quarter, but the dealer began to bluster and yell. Then with the sudden cynical self-analysis which I find so engaging, he remarked, "You shouldn't have paid me for the bookcase first. Let an Irishman have ten dollars in his pocket and he's rich, and wouldn't call the Pope his uncle."

So we left the coolness of the shop, and once more in the oven of the street Henry mourned, "I wanted that book for you. It was about Mexico and South America. We'll come back when the money's spent."

So we had lobster-salad sandwiches, iced tea and ice cream at the Waldoboro Tavern, with no more once-upon-a-times until we were again driving home by the long route through Winslow Mills.

"Once upon a time," said I, baiting my hook of thought as I put on a pair of gray glasses against the hot glare of the country seen without the protection of a car top.

There was a moment's pause.

"Here's a Chippendale one," said Henry. "Once upon a time a man fell through a well right into the sky above China, but fortunately a tree in the Imperial gardens broke his fall, though it is immemorially to be regretted that his eyeglasses, falling wide, broke off the honorable tip of the nail of the little finger of the Heir Apparent's right hand."

We entered the woods and their green shade.

"Once upon a time there was a clump of grass that thought it was hair so it combed itself every morning and died in the insane asylum," Henry said.

"It's a special gift," I thought, and went on to myself: "Once upon a time there was a little girl who cried and cried and cried," but my thought went no further.

We came out on the main road and turned back along the lower end of the lake, past the farm that keeps sheep whose cries we hear sometimes at dusk when the wind is right.

"Once upon a time there was a pencil that wanted to be a fountain pen and thinking that it couldn't, it cried and cried and cried and cried, and made a very good one indeed."

"You've been picking my brains," I said, "only mine was a little girl who cried and cried."

"Well," said Henry obligingly, easing the car over the solid rock ridge that juts out of the road above the sawmill hill where the wood lilies grow so bright in late summer: "Once upon a time there was a little girl and *she* cried and cried and cried and cried so her parents died young and she didn't have to wear diapers."

We were near home. More hills, and as we coasted down through wavering fields shaking in a hot wind, he went on.

"Once upon a time a hill wanted to run like a river and so it left its firm foundations and slid down upon itself, and overwhelmed three goats, seven rabbits and a fish peddler."

Past our neighbors', our own stone walls appear in sight and the game is ended.

"Once upon a time a little tree wouldn't take good advice and insisted upon growing downwards, but it realized its mistake for it reached the center of the earth where everything is molten and was scorched severely."

Home, with Bos'n panting and wagging his tail at us and Meg in overalls running to meet us, and Olga hurrying to get us iced grape juice with a plate of cake to be enjoyed in the parlor, and there were no more stories to be told.

THE BOOK OF MY CONTENT

"Lou souleil me fai canta," the Provençal poets say, and I, too, am a cicada and the sun makes me sing. A deep distrust of life warns me that this is my summer, every happy moment of it, not one of which must be wasted by not being recognized. I know my happiness and raise my voice in instinctive praise, catching the warmth about me. The psychologists say that the unspoken thing eats deeply, but for me it is often the spoken thing. Finding words for an experience will write it into the memory. This is the book of my content, catching here and there a cupful from all the happiness that pours past me. I find there are not many thoughts or ideas in it. The truth is, such things seem unimportant to me now. I wonder how it ever was that I was a junior Phi Beta Kappa, and laid such store by learning from books. Now I sit with Pussy in my arms and idly brood over the landscape and feel deep springs filling, which come straight from the heart of the earth and have little to do with the tindery excitement of abstractions.

Last evening we were driving home in the late afternoon from Damariscotta, the back of Fore-and-Aft filled with groceries and meats and a twenty-five pound bag of flour. The top was up because it had been showering, but as we drove by the wide smooth waters of the salt river, the sun burned out, and set the birch woods on the further bank to gleaming in a warm, gold, unreal light, while a thunderhead behind in the northeast turned to quiet puffs of rose and gold, serene on a sky that never was. It seemed like a painting of the romantic school that nature had copied. It affected me with the sadness of music. We drove on and stopped at the brow of the hill and watched longer. The shadow of the earth had darkened the landscape to a grave Indian look of pine woods and deep green velvet farmlands, serious against the glow of clouds heaped behind them. Slowly we watched the shadow of the earth like a blue fog creep up and up the bright pyramid of light, and at last we drove on, past hedges of ripening elderberry, to the farmhouse and a late supper.

THE CENTER OF THE UNIVERSE

After Henry had been in the hospital for pneumonia, the hardening of his arteries fastened upon him so that it was necessary for
him to have three nurses a day. Still, it was a cheerful household.
Henry never complained as his weakness increased. He laughed
as much as ever and once in a while he made a brilliant remark
like a sudden star seen through a cover of clouds. The nurses were
delightful. We had a housekeeper, and a gardener who may not
have known much about gardening but who could take Henry for
a drive when he felt like taking a drive, and could help him with
great gentleness when he needed to be lifted.

It was a pleasant household but I was almost never alone. And
now and then one has to be. At such times I would walk down
the long slope of our hayfield past the wild apple tree, to the
little dock near which our canoe had been moored. Walking halfway out along it I would sit down, cross-legged, watching the
water.

Water is something which repays almost endless watching.
Constantly it throws up reflected changing lights from its ripples,
and the same lights move along the shallow bottom. Dragonflies
cling to the reeds by the shore, long-legged insects walk on the
water, little bugs eddy about on its surface. Once, and only once,
I saw a young spider arrive on a long spider thread on which he
had pioneered westward with the wind, traveling the mile or so
across the pond.

The silence was almost unbroken except by an occasional bird,
or an even more occasional chipmunk running across the minus-

cule beach. The fish that went by were not very exciting. A six-inch bass was a monster. What I waited for was the long ribbon of young alewives whose parents had suffered the terrible struggle up the fish ladder which connects the salt-water river with the fresh-water lake at the Mills, so that these millions of tiny fish might be born in the ancestral fresh pond. They always made a band eighteen or twenty inches wide and swam two or three feet out from the shore, clockwise. Why clockwise? And always? I never saw them stop to eat, but if a larger fish swam up to their march to eat *them*, as sometimes happened, they would scatter like sparks of fire, spattering up out of the water only to re-form when the danger was over. Once I saw an alewife land on the grassy bank above the pond. It lay completely motionless for as long as a fish safely can and then, assuming that its enemy was gone, methodically flopped its way back into the pond. Or at least I assume that it was capable of assumption.

I never took a book to read. I suppose I wanted to avoid all action. Sitting cross-legged halfway down the little dock, I felt held in the sun's palm. That particular spot was the center of the universe. I sat quite quiet at the hub of the spinning galaxies.

Journeys in My Mind

1968–

§ Our lives followed the usual pattern. Our children, Margaret and Catherine—Meg and Kate—grew up and married; each has four children. Henry and I began to avoid "mud time" at the farm by going to California in March, for five or six weeks. We had rooms at the vanished Claremont College Inn, hired a small car and explored the countryside, often going up to Kate and Dick's for coffee after lunch. As time went on, Henry became more and more crippled by hardening of the arteries and the last four years of his life saw us at the farm all the year round, with Henry at first using a wheelchair and later staying mostly in bed attended by nurses round the clock. Almost until the very end he would go driving for a change, and I remember that a week before he died he asked to go out in the wheelchair to be under the sky. Of all the natural things he had so loved, the love of the sky remained with him to the end.

Since Henry's death eight years ago I have had no desire to travel. I used to visit my sister in Hingham three or four times a year for a few days at a time, but since her death three years ago I take only relatively short drives.

The long urge to write poetry has died almost completely away. And I live one day at a time.

BOUNDARIES

My chair is in the southeast corner of the living room flanked by a small bird's-eye maple table to the left and a nest of wicker French stools to the right. The telephone is on the wall at my side, with the especial amplifier to counteract my deafness.

The chair is a small upholstered armchair, the gift of my sister on that last Christmas, when I admired one like it beside her bed. It seems more like a good horse than a chair. It responds to every motion of the rider, it turns to left or right at the first shift of position, it rocks forward or backward as one leans a little this way or that. Wasn't it General Burnside who announced, "My headquarters will be in the saddle"?—to which Lincoln is said to have remarked, "It will be enough if he keeps his hindquarters there"? Anyway, my headquarters are certainly in this chair. My desk is a double piece of cardboard about eighteen inches by twelve, which I keep out of sight behind my chair leaning against the wall when it is not in use. Breakfast and lunch are served here on a tray, and my papers are kept in a basket which we found in the house when we bought it forty-three years ago, one of the several Indian kitchen baskets that used to be sold from door to door.

Earlier in the year when I came into this room a little after seven o'clock, it was filled with sunlight. Now that the sun has gone so far north the room is in the shadow of the house. The sun does not reach it until early afternoon, although the windows show a sunlit landscape. I should perhaps be out on the open verandah at the back, but writing outdoors takes a certain energy which I no longer have.

My sister used to call this a "busy" room. The carpet is a soft green but the wallpaper, which we put on when we first came here, is one that Henry chose. It came from a factory in Alsace. There are stripes of roses, a wide stripe alternating with a narrow one. The colors have not so much faded as mellowed. The large eighteenth-century armchair is upholstered in chintz. The other chairs and the sofa are in plain colors. Henry bought a what-not to put between the front windows, and the things on it have come from all parts of the world.

When our daughters were setting up their first houses I gave them the Persian rugs I had had in Shipcote, the old house in Hingham, but now I have a few of my sister's. She loved rugs and knew them, which I do not, but there is a beautiful one here at my feet. Our elder daughter, Meg, has sent me from Alaska, where she is now living, many Eskimo soapstone carvings, especially of seals and birds. Our younger daughter, Kate, lives in California within reach of a small shop which handles things from remote parts of South America. These textiles are both beautiful and brilliant and are scattered about the room.

The walls are covered with paintings, the smallest is on glass, framed in a wide border of horn (I cannot imagine what sort of horn was used). It shows a court lady at her dressing table attended by her maid. I bought it when I was sixteen in the Mexico City of those splendid flamboyant years before the revolutions, and carried it back in my suitcase with a funerary urn (shaped like a god) from Monte Alban, which had not yet been excavated.

I shan't go on, but the room has too many things in it and I couldn't get on without any of them. Each one reminds me of some person or place which I have loved. I am aware of them all, and they are companions sharing the many hours I spend with them. For Mrs. Ball, my housekeeper, leaves the house soon after breakfast and doesn't return until after five in the afternoon, which in winter time is black as midnight. One year the farms on either side of me were empty. I had the acres of pine wood on my west and the pond below me on the east for my only company.

But one morning I woke up thinking, "I *will* get that poodle puppy." My subconscious had decided during the night, remembering perhaps that Henry had always said, "There should be life along the floor." So I telephoned and bought the puppy, sight unseen and four months old, a handsome black standard puppy whom—yes, whom I named Tamar, after the ancestress who left Teesdale in the north of England and came to America with four of her married sons and their wives in 1817. "Tammy" we call her, and the house has never been empty since she came. At first she was a great deal of trouble, being independent as a pig on ice, but now she understands and takes part in the daily routine as much as any of us. And she is young, just five in April when I was eighty-three in May, and all the time she grows more loving. But her eyes can still sparkle with mischief and she can still race about the lawn in circles like a mad thing and throw herself bodily into the ice pools which form on the lawn in March. On the coldest day, I have never seen her shiver.

[From my window]

> I have no impulse to write poetry
>   except to say
> that on March 6, 1968, spring
>   came to the East Neck Road
>   in Nobleboro, Maine.
> It didn't come with a crocus,
> it didn't come with a robin,
> it didn't come with a melting
>   of all the snow.
> No, the children brought it
>   from one end of the road
>   to the other
> by hanging old lard pails and
>   glass milk bottles
>   on the maple trees.
> Every year they tap them. I
>   can't think they make
>   much syrup.
> Their kitchens can't be papered
>   or the paper would come off
>   in the steam
> as a stamp comes off an envelope
>   held over the kettle spout
> (in these days stamps come off
>   without any such bother).
> But somehow, for some reason of
>   their own,
> the children have brought back the spring
> and the good patient old maples are helping them.

THE POND

To the west we have the forests that other people would call woodlots, and our little mountains that are singularly blessed with unexpected cliffs and great knobs of stone from which we could see far off to the head of the lake and its blue hills. To our east, the hayfields slope down to the pond and the sunrise. All three farms on our Neck have the same geography: the houses are built in hayfields, and face to the south.

Damariscotta Pond, nowadays often called "Lake Damariscotta" although the old name persists in East Pond Road, lies in three sections. The largest is at Jefferson, where a beguiling stream enters it, and is so much the largest body of water that the people of Jefferson used to call it Jefferson Pond (but this the rest of the pond and the cartographers considered effrontery). It is part of Damariscotta Pond ending in the Narrows, which widen again into a section with several islands below Bunker Hill, where one loop runs down to Damariscotta Mills and its waterfalls. (In the old days this was called Damariscotta Fresh River, but I haven't heard the name used for years.) The final section curves about the two headlands of West Neck and East Neck and is called Muscongus Bay, which in Abnaki means "Bay of Thunders." (There is another Muscongus Bay on the Medomak River that passes through our next-door neighbor, Waldoboro.)

It is on our Muscongus Bay that we look out, and strangers think it a lake itself with its narrow pine-masted Loon Island and the very small round island which Henry used to call Pint

Pot (I don't know its real name). Between the islands the water shallows and the ice may be unsafe, as a neighbor across the pond discovered when driving home a team of horses after working in the woods on this side. The ice gave way and the poor horses were drowned, but the man saved himself because he was walking behind them by the length of the reins.

We see many delightful sights on the pond. In the early days we saw a yoke of oxen dragging some logs over the ice to the sawmill at Butter-and-Eggs Bridge at the foot of our pond (the sawmill is only a memory today). We have seen ice boats, and sail boats, and power boats pulling water-skiers. Occasionally we see a fleet of canoes from the boys' camp on West Neck. There is usually a pair of loons nesting on Loon Island and duck and even geese sometimes stop at our cove during migration. One year there were otter living in our little stretch of swampland, and we came upon the joyous track of one when we were snow-shoeing after a fresh fall of snow. There were the prints of paws for a very short distance and then a longer slide, and then the prints and then another slide.

Twice we have had beaver build bank-houses along the railroad at the bottom of the pond beyond Butter-and-Eggs Bridge, and twice they have been evicted and their house torn down, but all along our shores there are the marks of their woodcutting enter-prises. A neighbor was said to have kept his kitchen stove going most of the year by using the lengths of beaver wood he collected from his shore.

Next door to us, and also with a wonderful view down the pond, there is a large, well-kept farm to whose kitchen I so often went for milk and eggs. The window above the sink looked out over the pond and if I asked the farmer's wife, as I often did, "What's the weather going to be, Mrs. Rollins?" she would first glance at the island to see on which side the slick appeared. She never bothered to look at a weathervane, though they had two of them. From childhood the island had been vane enough. Having seen from which direction the wind was coming, a glance at the sky was enough to determine her answer, and a very good weather prophet she was. As is her daughter today, but she judges the wind more from the trees and the movement of the leaves than from the island.

I think of Mrs. Rollins at her sink and Louise, her daughter, as old women, but I am older than either of them, here as I sit writing on my piece of cardboard in my little brown chair in the corner of the living room. But as I write about past times, I am part of them, not of this circumscribed Today. The pond is something I explore with Henry—in canoe, or swimming, or on snowshoes—not something at which I glance from the open verandah or a window. For so many years it was part of my life, not part of my view!

GHOSTS

I have never believed in ghosts, and still do not, but of late years I have seen two. They were completely unterrifying and completely different. The first one I saw when taking a cruise down the Great Lakes with Henry. Our Canadian cruise ship was following one of the long stretches of river between two lakes, and we were passing what seemed an endless swamp of tussocks and tamarack trees, both of the same ugly khaki color. Of a sudden we came to a small solitary shack facing on the river. It was painted the same khaki as the swamp and the tamarack trees. It was empty, with the open front door and the downstairs window beside and the one above it showing as black oblongs. It was a basic house: roof, walls, two windows and a door, like a terrible doll-house.

I was sitting by myself on the deck watching, and as we went very slowly by it I thought about the man who had built it, deciding that he might have been a fisherman or a muskrat-trapper, and then I thought of the utterly lonely life of the woman who may have shared this gaunt shell of a house with him. And I thought, "He would have had something to do, but what was *her* life like?" and as I thought hard about her and the horror of her life a shape all at once appeared in the black rectangle of the door. It was white as salt and had the outline of a sarcophagus, a head-shape set on shoulders that tapered down to the feet. It leaned a little against the doorjamb, just slightly to one side of dead center. It did not stir. It was not there, but then, very bright and clear, it was there. I don't know how long I stared at it before it was gone, snuffed out as sud-denly as it had appeared, and there was only the black oblong of the doorway left.

So much for my vision of an ectoplasm (or so I am told), featureless, motionless and unforgettable. My second ghost ap-peared to me some years later on my way back to my sister's at Hingham from a visit with Louise Bechtel in Mount Kisco. It was the longest trip I had taken in many years and I found the new highways difficult to follow, because driving at seventy miles an hour I was only aware of the meaning of a sign after I had passed it. But Susan Hirschman, then the editor of children's books at Macmillan, a department of which Louise had been first editor (and indeed the first editor of a separate department of children's books in the world) was giving a cocktail party at Macmillan in Louise's honor to mark the fiftieth anniversary of her first taking office. The day after the party I was returning to my sister's in Hingham. The car needed more gasoline and I was anxious not to get off the highway, and I remembered that through Hartford the town came right up to the road, so as we neared the outskirts I began scanning the skyline for the high signs to be found at most stations. *Motel—Motel—Motel* I read, and suddenly *Esso—Esso* very bright and high. I swung off the highway to my right into a large parking lot and drove up to the gas pumps. Glancing further to my right I saw a man's figure walking towards me. He was middle-aged and had none of the smart appearance of modern station attendants, but looked like many I used to see, a dark, stubbly-faced man in an old sweater with his belt fastened under his paunch. I turned to roll down the lefthand window to speak to him when he came up.

But nothing happened. I waited and then turned back to the parking lot. It was empty. No man was approaching and there were no cars nor trucks parked there, nor any other obstruction. Only then did I look directly ahead of me at the neat building with its *For Sale* sign across the window.

At the next station I was told that the Esso complex had been closed for about a year, and the boy I talked with had no idea who had owned it.

This was my matter-of-fact ghost. Could it be that mine was the first car to have blundered up to the pump in that year? Did my action trigger an old routine, and my expectation of finding an attendant there, draw one to the spot from nothingness? I don't explain my ghosts; but still, though I saw both clearly, and without the least fear, I don't believe in ghosts.

REFLECTIONS

Mirrors are strange things. A pool of unruffled water served our ancestors, or water in a pail or bowl. Later polished silver or steel took the place of water. Now we have looking-glasses.

But there is something dangerous about mirrors. They contain and perhaps retain the images of the people who have looked into them. To break one is to bring seven years of bad luck, perhaps because it is a kind of murder, or at least of suicide: the long line of images which the mirror has held demand their revenge. Everyone knows that Plato himself wrote an epigram on how Laïs, who had "laughed exultant over Greece" for so many years, hung up her mirror in the Temple of Aphrodite "since such as I am I will not see myself, and such as I was I cannot."

Queen Elizabeth had the mirrors in her palaces covered as she grew old. She is not remembered as a beauty but she was often told that she was one. She more than once tried to get a Scots ambassador to compare her with Queen Mary, her cousin. Elizabeth, too, had white skin and bright eyes set off by the jewels she wore, but the ambassador always fobbed her off with a diplomatic answer, and proudly and rather pathetically she would ask the same question of some other man who had seen both queens. When she grew old she had every mirror covered. Then, as with Laïs, she feared to see the present compared with the past.

When I was young and lucky enough to receive a compliment, I'd say, "Oh, wait until I'm eighty! Then I *shall* be handsome!" This was because I thought my Grandmother Coatsworth was, and I had the idea that our family, like brandy, improved with age.

My mirror doesn't think so. And that reminds me of mirrors and death. Why did they always cover the mirrors in a house when someone had died? Did they think that the spirit would be so enamored of its new appearance that it would hang about indefinitely? Or that it would receive a shock at seeing itself as it was? Or did they think that as the body must be buried, so the ten thousand reflections of that body must go through a ritual burial too? If the mirrors were not veiled, would ghosts of the dead person detach themselves from it and wander about? How many people would walk this house if they could rise from the mirrors that have reflected them—some of my own blood and dear to me, and some that would be utter strangers.

What dynamite we handle when we lift a mirror or bend towards one! I seldom do.

SECOND ADOLESCENCE

People used to speak of "a second childhood" where now they say "senile." That stage I have not reached, though I can feel the presence of a shadowy second adolescence. I have more daydreams than for many years I had time for, but usually now they are in the form of memories, not longings. I forget words (the other day I came to a full stop because I had lost "button" from my mind), and generally use a synonym because I know that any word is better than none. I forget names, but I comfort myself with the knowledge that I have always forgotten them. The long-ago day comes back to me when a stranger asked me my name—I was perhaps six—and the sudden question drove it entirely from my mind. I still remember the bewildered feeling of "I don't know who I am"; and perhaps I still feel it.

My body, which was never beautiful or athletic, sufficed me nicely. Now it betrays me continually in small ways. But so far I have been spared arthritis and most of the other painful companions of old age. I am hampered by deafness, in one ear I think, but perhaps in both. (Is that inherited? I can remember Father saying in his forties, "Oh, that won't keep me awake—I'll lie on my good ear.") Whether inherited or not, it hampers me. I have a hearing aid but so far have not learned how to use it properly. Often when I wear it I shout, matching my voice, I suppose, to the voice I hear which is louder than normal.

I cannot walk any distance, and have to beware of losing my balance. Oh, the falls I have had! In the most notable fall, three or four years ago, I broke my right hip, though I didn't know it until finally, ten days later, I had it X-rayed. It healed without an operation after I spent three months in my own bed at home, using a walker when I had to move around. It isn't because of the hip that I stump along, leaning forward to watch where I am going; that's hardening of the arteries and is very limiting, but not at all painful.

At eighty-three I drive a car, but I don't like to go for long distances. Four years ago, when my sister Margaret was alive, I thought nothing of driving two hundred miles to stay with her three or four times a year; now I doubt that I could do it. When I no longer have a license I shall be a toad-in-a-hole indeed.

A generation or two ago there were people who were able to say from the heart, "It is God's will," and there are still a few such people. I wish that I might be one of them! To me, I appear to be no more in the universal scale than an old leaf still clinging to the bough before dropping and making way for other leaves. But I am lucky so far to have "retained my faculties." I still think; I still write; I still read: I still see my friends—and still have some, heaven be praised! to see.

These remarks are necessarily self-centered, but not by intention. They are written primarily for people of my own age or for those who are approaching it, to discuss honestly the problems which we all face. It is my good fortune to have inherited, nothing so dashing as courage, but acceptance of what cannot be changed, and a willingness to enjoy the small gifts of life which still are so plentiful if one will look for them.

PASTIMES

All my life I have read: romances, books of travel, books of theory—usually what are called "good books," well written by established authors. But with Henry's illness and even more since his death, the level of my reading has declined. Now I read almost entirely mystery and detective stories. I go in and out of Nero Wolfe's house with Archie, I visit southern France and Greece with Mary Stewart, I go back with pleasure to Buchan. Of course Agatha Christie's books, uneven though they are, form a backbone, and with them *The Nine Tailors* and the other Lord Peter Wimsey tales, and Helen MacInnes and many, many others. I don't touch James Bond, because he was sadistic. My murdered people are usually dead when the story begins or die suddenly from a blow or a shot, without fear or pain.

Of course the books are usually exciting, but more than that they are the last stand of the old-fashioned novel. They have characters and plots. They begin, they come to a crisis, they end with an untying of the complexities of the situation which they have built up so carefully. Their detectives are heroes, or at least sufficiently heroes for my purpose, a relief after the non heroes of modern fiction and the non-action, too, for that matter. I am old, and I like the older fashions in writing.

When I was young I should have thought the books I now read a waste of time. Now that I wish to make the days short, they are ideal for my purpose. They are pastimes in the full meaning of the word. I am tired of playing Patience. I have friends but I am very careful not to ask too much of them (and how generously they give without being asked!), but a book could be written, and very likely has been, on how to be a widow gracefully. I am sure such a book would suggest that one join various groups or clubs, or now the Senior Citizens. I can't do it. Neither Henry nor I was a joiner.

WE ARE ALL LIKE ICEBERGS

The only iceberg I ever saw was the one in the Straits of Belle Isle, and sailing down the outer coast of Newfoundland and up the coast of Labrador we saw no more of them. That one iceberg was like all the descriptions of icebergs I have read. It was pinnacled and shining and was sapphire blue in its shadows. But the most important thing about it was that nine tenths of it we didn't see at all.

I sometimes realize that we are all like icebergs. The important part of us that determines our behavior lies in the subconscious beneath the waterline of awareness. I am content with others and with myself to leave it there, yet as I grow older I become aware that certain of my own characteristics, which I never connected with one another, spring from some single source.

The one I have in mind is that I am badly co-ordinated. As a child I continued to talk "baby talk" until I went to school. "Ne-pa-to" indeed! What way is that for a four- or five-year-old girl to ask for a "needle to sew"? Only Margaret, three years older than I, could interpret my language to the family, which was amused but not at all concerned.

By the time I reached school I could talk so that I could be understood, but the next evidence of my particular weakness was shown in my not being able to sing. I could hear a tune perfectly well, and later on I could detect the slightest flatting in concert singing. But the connection between ear and vocal cords was poor. Invariably I sang off-key. So did my father and his mother. It was not considered strange that I could neither sing nor play the piano.

This lack of co-ordination ran, unnoticed, through all my life. I never played the skilled games, tennis or golf or even bridge. I walked, canoed, rode, swam in an old-fashioned way, and snowshoed. I liked the outdoors, but approached it in a rudimentary manner. I can recognize most of the birds at the feeding station, but I do not recognize their songs when I hear them.

This weakness is very marked in my social life and has always been so. I do not remember names and I don't recognize faces. I might recall what someone had said ten years earlier, yet pass that person on the street without a smile. I can only imagine what people have said, and still must say, about me. I sometimes wonder if it *is* indifference on my part. I don't think so.

I am the last person to learn the name of a new disease, of a foreign author, of an unusual flower, of any scientific discovery. Yet from the first grade through graduate school at the university I was an honor student. This difficulty with words has had a strong effect upon my writing. I have, quite deliberately, tried to make my writing clear rather than rich. And as always happens when one chooses one path instead of another, I have lost by the choice as well as gained.

※

CALL IT MY ANGEL

Most writers find it difficult to start off on a book or even an article. Many smoke cigarettes or drink an extra cup of coffee or rearrange their papers.

"Make a beginning," says my good angel.

"I thought I'd pay bills and write letters this morning," I say hastily.

"They can wait," says my angel. "Make a beginning. It need be only a sentence."

"But the first sentence is very important."

"Write it then. You need write nothing more this morning if you don't want to. It will only take a minute."

"And you won't insist on more?"

"I never insist," says my good angel.

I get out my notebook, a lined composition book from the five-and-ten-cent store, and the ballpoint pen which I prefer to the pencils Henry used, although they gave him an excuse to sharpen them very often when his work was going slowly.

Pen in hand I write a sentence, rather at random.

In some part of the world, in Africa, I think, they have a proverb: "One cloud is lonely." It may or it may not be true of clouds, but it certainly is true of sentences. Out of pure pity I write a second sentence to be company to the first. And then I am done for. I write a third and a fourth and soon I am hard at work. My good angel stands apart and makes no suggestions even when I follow a dead end and have to cross out several pages.

"Yes, that wasn't good," she agrees, reading over my shoulder. But that day she makes no suggestions. She is not a bit of help.

The next morning she is there to do a little urging to get me started. Then she goes off and stares out the window. The ground is bare of snow and khaki-colored, and all the birds and the possible chipmunks are on the other side of the house under the century-and-a-half-old apple tree. I can't imagine what she finds to look at all morning.

This may go on for a good many days, but sooner or later she becomes really interested in the story as it evolves on the lined paper. Her hand softly descends on mine—I could scarcely say at what moment of time it happens—but now she is writing, using my hand as I use my ballpoint pen. I am often surprised by the ideas and details she puts in. They had not occurred to me when I was sketching out the general scheme of the work in bed the night before.

If I speak of the additions she smiles and says, "Hush," and goes on writing with my hand. I am elated. All I have to do is to be passive. She is in full control.

But at last, sometimes sooner, sometimes later, she lifts her hand from mine.

"Now finish," my good angel says.

"But that's the hardest part," I protest, dependent after so much assistance.

"Then it's high time you tackle it," she says, going to her stand by the window.

There is nothing for me to do but to finish the story as best I may, knowing that the editors will probably not be satisfied with it.

"Now go over the whole thing and correct it," she says over her shoulder.

"But the parts you wrote don't need correcting," I say.

My good angel turns briskly to face me. "Nonsense! My writing is no better than yours. It is only easier for you, that is all."

"But you——" I begin.

" 'But I,' " she mocks me; and adds: "You know perfectly well that by whatever name you call me, I am only your subconscious."

Then my good angel smiles. "Call me whatever muse you like. It doesn't alter what I am."

This is the usual course of writing a book. It was so with my latest story, which appeared in 1975, suggested by a Hebridean legend but translated onto a Maine island setting. But the book written the year before—*All-of-a-Sudden Susan*—my angel would have no part in. She had no criticisms to make. She was just never in the room when I brought it out to work on. She did not even glance over my shoulder when it was done. But once or twice I thought I felt her give me a nudge. Even of that I am not quite sure.

LIFE ALONG THE FLOOR

Human beings have diluted our instincts with too much thinking; we are pulled this way and that and it is often hard for us to come to a simple decision. I think that four-footed animals act much more instinctively and that their instincts are usually right for them. This is why I like to watch them in their less complicated world. They are individuals and often confused like ourselves, but I still feel that they are fundamentally wiser than we. When Tammy spends a hot summer day mostly flat on her side in a doorway I feel justified in stopping work and picking up a book.

THE SUN IS A COMPANION

Each decade that I have lived has had its especial joys and difficulties. Now I take a piercing delight when I am alone in the afternoons just looking about the room in which I sit. The farmhouse is very quiet. Probably Tamar is asleep in a patch of sunlight on the floor. But the rooms are silent. No foot falls overhead, there is no stir outside the door.

Tranquillity and delight come flooding in with the sunlight. I do not feel this happiness on rainy days. But the sun is a companion. It lies across the furniture I know so well, across the long rose Persian rug that was my sister's, it touches the forsythia and pussy-willow wands in the big bowl on the low wicker table below the west window, it lights up an Eskimo soapstone carving of seals, or burns on a San Blas Indian pillow in one of the chairs. The room is filled with things, too many, but every one of them sings to me, of the giver or of the place from which it has come. The delight that I used to take in traveling has narrowed down to this small focus, but it is still as eager and as pure as when I ranged the world. Shall I ever forget when Henry and I looked up and saw Chichen Itza like a great white dream city in the jungle? Shall I forget how Margaret and I watched lobsters crawling beneath us from a wharf north of the Cabot Trail on Cape Breton? It is a long time since New Englanders have seen lobsters only a few feet from the beach.

I have a thousand memories. I could, I suppose, travel still, but so cautiously and in such a diminished world! I am content to remember larger times. The world in which I live is enough for me. After so many travels, I am home, and my happiness here is no less than it was in foreign lands and my sense of wonder has not dulled with all these years. I am as happy as an old dog stretched out in the sunlight. I remember other times, other places, but (in the sunlight) I am content with here and now.

KNOWLEDGE

When I was young I had a passion for learning things. I was like a jackdaw, and all information looked to me bright as tin to be carried away to my nest. I loved books and study and learned quickly so that I never had to be what we then called a grind, for heaven had granted me the gift of concentration, a boon indeed to any child during those long years of school. I remember that on the first day of school when Mother led me into the big room on the lower floor of the Franklin School on Park Street in Buffalo my attention was caught by a pair of beaded moccasins on the wall, and a prism scattering rainbows from where it hung fastened to a window shade. I had seen moccasins before and they took my imagination, but the prism breaking white light into rainbows was new to me, and it is probably not by accident that I had them on the four shades of the parlor at Shipcote. Truly I was to travel far on the trail of books and there was always to be a rainbow lighting it for me.

And yet as I grow older I have suffered a curious revulsion of feeling and I do not very much like to think of my school days. True, my first eight years of school at the Franklin were Spartan. We followed a modified British model, with Latin in the fifth grade and French in the seventh. We were drilled unremittingly and stayed almost daily after school learning poetry by heart for the smallest infringement of rules. Even a borrowed pencil set us to learning poetry after the school bell had rung at last. The training was thorough, but I am not thorough.

Later I went for two years to a school in Pasadena kept by an old Scotswoman and an old Frenchwoman with an Irish name. We studied on long verandahs under vines at the back of the building. At this time I had a sort of contempt for the school because no girl had ever gone from it to college, and the math teacher sometimes made a mistake in the algebra problem she was demonstrating on the blackboard. Now I am not so sure that my attitude should not have been one of admiration for the humane reasonableness of the tradition there. My last two years before college were spent at the big new building of the Buffalo Seminary just across the parkway from our house, and there we had merriment and serious work mixed and I went to Vassar well prepared. Perhaps too well prepared, for much of my first year repeated work I had already done, and I lost the eagerness of my will to study, and never wholly regained it.

But after seventeen years of study in school and college I never noticed from what direction the wind was blowing. I didn't know what to do for a burn, or the names of any but the commonest flowers. I could not have recognized a bird song, or gone to market and made a wise selection. I could not hem, judge a person's character; and I didn't know the names of the streets which I had passed by daily for years. For what was I educated? To be a teacher? But I never became a teacher, and what wisdom did I have to impart for all the books I had read? To be a writer? Perhaps. But I have learned to forget all I studied. I have more respect for one thing faithfully observed than for a thousand learned from another man's mind. Is this the Rousseau mood? It is so long since I glanced over *The New Heloïse* that I'm not sure, but I think he held that information was not very valuable in itself.

Obviously this is an emotional reaction, not to be very seriously considered. But I find that I have a vast respect for close observation and an independently arrived-at conclusion. A world in which newspaper headlines and editorial opinions, or television news, or articles compressed from magazines for monthly digests form the basis of the intellectual pabulum is not very interesting. Most conversations are little better than quotations without quotation marks. It has always been more or less true, but in the past the catchwords were more often handed down than around, and they took on a salt and pithiness, as they passed from generation to generation, which today's speech lacks.

PLAIN POEMS

On December 14, 1968, good or bad, for the first time for many
months the old fervor was with me as I wrote. Good or bad, it is
poetry, not verse.

I am always mislaying things nowadays
my glasses, my pen, a book.
They were here a moment ago
            until this malice possessed them.
I will find them perhaps where I left them
or perhaps never find them at all.
But there are more important things
            mislaid everywhere:
glimpses of beauty, moments of pity,
            sudden recollections,
intonations, the shadows of clouds,
            half-heard sounds,
passing, passing, already beyond reach,
lost while I look for my glasses,
gone, as I telephone.

          *   *   *

Oh what a clumsy awkward muse
          you are who have befriended me!
When you walk out of the woods your feet
          are muddy, your cheeks are thorn-scratched.
When you rise from the water, you rub
          your eyes and wring out your wet hair.
When you come from the sky it is
          like the landing of a crane,
legs outstretched before you, long wings
          braking.
There is nothing aërial or nymph-like
          about you,
the naiads are not your sisters.
But how glad I am to see you,
          I who was deserted!
How you bring with you the smell
          of the woods, the smell of water
the smell of the wind when rain is coming!

*   *   *

This is a song to March, a gloomy song.
My sister says March is a wonderful month,
never again will the skies be so beautiful.
She says you can tell that the sap
                is rising in the trees,
the twig tips redden and under the softening earth,
the roots confer with new grasses
                and opening flowers,
the earth awakens from its winter sleep,
the quiet winter birds are now fighting
                for their mates,
you hear the sound of valiant scuffling everywhere.
But the country people know that this is
                the month of elimination
when the weak are cleared away: there is no place
                for them.
This is the month of death. The wise country people
call it March Hill, easy for the strong to climb,
                but the weak
die on its slopes: March the month of renewal
and the month of death.

*   *   *

To feel the old body dragging
                on the spirit's arm—
"Not so fast, not so fast, I am tired."
To see the old body stumbling
                as it walks,
breathing heavily, peering
                uncertainly,
asking for a comfortable seat—
what a humiliation!
Soon enough the spirit will
                leave the old body at home—
"You want to stay put! Stay put
                then! I'm off!"
"Possibly," mumbles the old body.
                "And possibly not."

                  *   *   *

I can fall behind in the race,
I can sit down on a boulder
                by the road,
I can fall behind in the race,
breathe quietly, feeling my forehead
                grow cool again,
hear my heart stop its pounding.
I can fall behind in the race
and watch the others, as I might watch
                salmon swimming up a river.
What did they say the prize was?
I've forgotten.

                  *   *   *

The sun shines on the new-fallen snow,
is not that whiteness enough? No,
the snow must flash back in sequins,
the old goldenrod and milkweed stalks,
      all weeds and grasses,
are crystal along the road. Is that
      not enough?
No. The woods are white
      with hoar frost,
against the rising sun the glades
      and valleys shine in glory
and through this all I drive,
      looking solemn as an owl,
wearing only one glove.

    *   *   *

Oh the ties that bind mother
      and daughters together!
And the knots in the ties!
Sometimes our fingers meet
      as we try to untangle
      the cat's-cradle they make.
Untwist one string and we twist another.
Whose fault is it? Nobody's
      fault.
The ties are there. It is their
      nature to knot,
our nature to struggle with them.
And often our fingers touch.

    *   *   *

You pretty creatures flushed rose-white
with dawn
rising with lifted wings and curving necks
up from the cygnets hidden
in the leaves,
your silent and arrested flight
fills the whole room with
beauty,
clear and cool.
Dear cyclamen, dear swans,
let my dream hold you.

*   *   *

The sunlight on my bedroom wall
is my true calendar,
exact as an Aztec sundial.
I see it. I know what it is,
but I have never learned
to read it.

*   *   *

Wordsworth, Coleridge and Thoreau
        often composed poetry as
        they walked.
Wordsworth composed, pacing the
        bordered paths in his garden
under the fruit trees. Coleridge
        liked better
to find his words as he scrambled
        up a hillside through the
        brambles,
and Thoreau chose
        his verses walking
        under the pines
or treading a freshly turned
        furrow, with one sharp eye
        on the lookout for arrowheads.
I, too, like to shape a poem as
        I walk
even on this black-top, back-
        country road,
and being, like Thoreau, an American,
I am always looking, waiting
        for some marvel
which never comes. But today
a dozen chickadees gathered in the
        trees about me as I stood catching
        my breath,
and darted and chittered from
        twig to twig,
ignored by the downy woodpecker and the little
        brown mouse of a creeper
already in possession.

            *   *   *

You might call it a blizzard,
anyhow it was snowing so hard that people had put on
        their headlights
and it was blowing too. Some
        of the lower trees looked like snowbanks.
I was happy to be out in it driving alone, an unasked-for
        adventure.
An appointment at the lab, and an appointment later with
        a doctor—that was all,
but they were exciting as cocktail parties once were.
I had changed my dress, I had left the house,
and now I was off to definite destinations through
        driving snow.
As it turned out, there was a bonus, a friend in a
        conical fox-fur cap
who joined me at the hospital snack bar for coffee and
        toasted English muffins
between appointments. It was a fine morning
and storming more wildly than ever as I drove slowly home again.

*   *   *

Walking alone along the empty road
a long staff in one mittened hand
my boots making only a dull whispering,
rabbit-skin cap pulled low, long black coat buttoned high,
I might be a character in a Tolstoy novel
with the pines and birch trees on one side of me
and the sun going down on the other,
white and rayless beyond the marsh
glittering a little on the edges of the rotten snow.
Tall, broad-shouldered, slow-moving
I might be a pilgrim making my heavy way to some shrine
where the ikons glitter through incense,
my thoughts darkening as I walk when a cloud darkens
          this countryside,
and my sins weighing like stones in my heart.
But if I am a character in a Tolstoy novel
I am not such a pilgrim, only some old peasant woman
slowly, silently, making my way from the fields homeward
where the pot of cabbage soup simmers on the fire.

*   *   *

Anyone can see at a glance
    that I am old.
I, I, alone do not see it.
When I look at myself in
    the mirror
I see a hundred selves,
even the child.
When I speak or act, anyone
    of them at all
may speak or act for me,
even the child.
Only of one thing I am sure:
when I dream
I am always ageless.

OH, THEN I SHOULD BE VERY

SELECTIVE!

A personality to be a work of art must first have quality and second be ruthlessly simplified. You must be able to say of such a one: "'The eighteenth century is his hobby" or "I never see squills without thinking of her." A personality must have recognizably distinct likes and dislikes on almost every side. If a few of these are unexpected, so much the better. The incongruity increases the charm. But in the feast that the world sets before the diner, a choice must have been made, the plates selected, the wines ordered.

In all this I am a lamentable failure. I can't dislike even gladioli whole-heartedly. I do not know who is my favorite author. My reputation as a cat-lover is accidental, for I like cats no more than other animals. I regard all politics with confusion, all theories with suspicion, all arts with interest. Out of this inchoate mass of feelings, only a few things emerge.

My favorite landscape is a long slope of desert circled by mountains in the late afternoon with the smell of sand and sage in the air.

My favorite fruit is raspberries.

I love the lonely ruins of civilizations.

And if I could paint I should paint nothing but pools of water and their reflections. As a writer, of course I write of every sort of thing. But if I were a painter, oh, then I should be very selective! You would come into my studio and find nothing there but studies of still water—not lakes, nor rivers, nor waves, but wet New York pavements mirroring street lamps and the bright inhuman reds and greens of taxicab lights; and the dark grave reflections of grass in the long puddles of country ruts; and rainwater glazed with clouds in the granite hollows of a rock pasture; and the faces of people reflected back, small and intense, from the deep girandole of a well.

THOSE OTHER LANDS

I have traveled in many lands, but the best I have never set foot in. My favorite is the empty country back of India, beyond Mongolia. Once there were large oases there and great cities, and solitary travelers find inscriptions in languages that no one can read. For hundreds of miles along the caravan trail runs the wall that the Chinese once built to guard the Silk Route. The watchtowers were raised in sight of one another's flares, and some of the iron baskets remain in which the beacons were burned and one or two have the charred remains of the last despairing fire which no one was left to respond to. When the trail crosses mountain ranges one finds people with blue eyes, who look like Swiss. They are a native type, not the descendants of Alexander's troops. You can see those too, or people who claim to be them, and the sculpture and frescoes of ruined buildings which are half Greek and half Oriental. All this you can see if you and your camels last out long enough and if your guides do not cut your throat. This world lies behind the Hindu Kush.

Then there is Greenland with its ruins of Viking farmsteads, its icebergs and ice floes—let alone "Greenland's icy mountains" —its deep fiords so green in summer and the mystery of the disappearance of its two Scandinavian colonies, the one to the north gone without sign of violence or any message, taking its church bells, precious for their iron perhaps, and leaving their flocks and herds still grazing untended. The disappearance of the larger western colony was slower. It lasted probably until after the voyages of Columbus. In the museum of Copenhagen I have seen coarse wool garments dug out of the permafrost near Cape Farewell, the most complete collection of the clothes of Chaucer's time anywhere in the world. And how small they look! They might have been left behind by trolls.

I have admired an iceberg castle in the Straits of Belle Isle, but my Greenland is one of the imagination.

I used to be fascinated by Africa and its peoples and its arts, but that fascination hasn't stayed the course. With the years I have become merely interested—very much interested, but no longer fascinated. In the Middle East only that part of Turkey with its many volcanic cones in which the pigeons congregate in old painted churches and dwellings carved out of the tufa, holds my fancy.

None of these places have I ever seen and certainly never will see. But I do not wish to see them. They swim in my fancy, often nameless. They are a living part of my thought.

I did not know travel at its dawn, as Marco Polo might have claimed, though he, too, had many predecessors. But it was at my dawn, and the early light lies on my memories. We never went on tours, or by schedule: we followed our whims, stayed for a day or a week or a month in one place, or struck off at a tangent when someone told of some wonder. Only once did some pilgrims to the high Buddhist monasteries of the Korean Diamond Mountains look at us in wonder as the first white people they had seen (and examined our clothing almost to our skin) but we traveled at a time when all ports did not look alike and when people, East and West, wore the clothes their ancestors had worn. I should never feel such joy traveling in today's homogenized world.

But in my armchair, I still travel. I have looked down on the bones of Sir John Franklin's valet who had almost reached the last Arctic encampment in which the remnants of the expedition died, one by one. And why are his bones so especially interesting and touching? Because he carried still in his skeleton hand the brush with which he was accustomed to brush his master's clothes after each day's terrible journey. Even in dying he had not laid down the symbol of his service.

In back-page corners of the newspapers one may still come on little notices that feed the imagination: perhaps a new tribe of Indians has been discovered in its hammocks in the Amazonian jungle; or an (almost) completely primitive group has been found in a cave on one of the Philippine Islands; or a volcanic island has risen from the sea off the coast of Iceland and the scientists are watching to see what will be the first living thing that will adapt itself to its inhospitable lava shores. For myself I choose the paragraph about the Korean sailor rescued at sea from the back of a great turtle. Unnoticed, he had fallen off his vessel, discovered the sea turtle not far off, and climbed onto its curved and plated shell. His rescuers were prepared to swear that they had found him in the open sea riding the sea turtle. The fact was not considered important enough to warrant details as to how long he had been there, why he had fallen off his ship in the first place, and what, if anything, he had had to eat and drink. Nor was any word vouchsafed as to what had happened to the turtle.

Through the windy night something
    is coming up the path
    towards the house.
I have always hated to wait for things.
    I think I will go
    to meet whatever it is.

A General Chronology

1893   Born at Buffalo, New York, daughter of William T. and Ida Reid Coatsworth.

1898–99 Abroad eight months in England, Germany, Switzerland, Italy and Egypt.

1906–09 First two years of high school, in Pasadena, California.

1908   Christmas–New Year's vacation in Mexico; January 1909 at Oaxaca.

1909–11 At the Buffalo Seminary.

1912   Father died, family gave up home in Buffalo.

1911–15 At Vassar College.

1914   During a summer's walking trip in England, E.C. "began to write poetry with real zest."

1915   B.A. Vassar, with Junior Phi Beta Kappa.

1916   Lived in New York. M.A. at Columbia University.

1916–18 Thirteen months in the Far East: Japan, China, the Philippines, Java, Siam; China again (to Peking and edge of the Gobi Desert), houseboat to West Lake. In Korea to Diamond Mountains, with 24 coolies. Japan; and final month in Hawaii.

      Before and after the Orient, lived with relatives in California.

1919   Sister, Margaret, married Morton Smith, and came East to live in Hingham, Massachusetts. E.C. and her mother lived in Cambridge, Massachusetts, where E.C. studied at Radcliffe.

1920–28 "Years of work and travel hard to untangle": with her mother and sister traveled in Normandy, Brittany, England and Scotland; later with mother and friends around the Mediterranean, returning to Egypt and on to the Holy Land. Journeys alternated between Europe and California.

In 1921 or 1922 her mother bought the house in Hingham called "Shipcote," which became their base until E.C.'s marriage.

1929 In January, E.C. became engaged to Henry Beston, author and naturalist. Spring in California—when she wrote Newbery Medal-winning *The Cat Who Went to Heaven*; rode on mule-back with Margaret into the mountains of Guatemala.

In June married Henry Beston, honeymoon at "The Fo'castle," celebrated in his classic *The Outermost House*.

1930 Daughter Margaret (Meg) born in June.

1931 Bought "Chimney Farm" at Nobleboro, Maine; thereafter moved to Maine.

1932 Daughter Catherine (Kate) born in April.

1933–54 Many trips with H.B.: to the Gaspé in 1933, to Yucatán and Mexico, Arizona and California in 1936–38, many trips to Canada for H.B.'s book *The St. Lawrence* (published 1942). With Meg and Kate to Denmark, Sweden, Norway in 1953; with Meg to Paris, Denmark, Sweden, and Iceland in 1954.

1953 Kate married Richard Barnes.

1956 Meg married Dorik Mechau.

1957–67 Spent winters mostly in Claremont, California; to Mexico in 1960. H.B. very ill in winter of 1960–61. By 1963, each daughter had four children.

1968 H.B. died on April 15 and was buried in the farm burying ground.

1968–86 E.C. lives at Chimney Farm with her housekeeper and black standard poodle, Tamar.

A Casual Index